# SHAKESPEARE MATTERS

Also available in the series:
*Latin Matters*

First published in the United Kingdom in 2008 by
Portico Books
10 Southcombe Street
London
W14 0RA

An imprint of Anova Books Company Ltd

ISBN 9781906032456

A CIP catalogue record for this book is available from the British Library.

10 9 8 7 6 5 4 3 2 1

Reproduction by Rival Colour Ltd., UK
Printed and bound by CT Printing Ltd., China

This book can be ordered direct from the publisher.
Contact the marketing department, but try your bookshop first.

www.anovabooks.com

# SHAKESPEARE MATTERS

## GEOFF SPITERI

*And seeing ignorance is the curse of God,*
*Knowledge the wing wherewith we fly to heaven*
— Lord Say, *Henry VI, Part II, Act IV, scene vii*

**PORTICO**

# INTRODUCTION

## DOES SHAKESPEARE MATTER?

In a recent survey commissioned for the National Year of Reading, teenagers were asked what their most and least favourite things to read were. Top of the popular list was gossip magazine *Heat!*, with online computer game cheats and *Harry Potter* not far behind. Top of the most loathed reads was homework, with the runner-up spot taken by the collected works of one William Shakespeare.

It's not only teenagers who feel like this about the Great Bard. For many of us, Shakespeare boils down to a few hazily remembered plots and one or two of the more famous lines that pretty much everyone can mis-quote. For most of us too, even just the mention of the author's name summons up memories of long, ardu-ous – if not downright boring – lessons spent in class-rooms attempting to translate arcane, 400-year-old words and phrases into modern English. For most of us the experience will have been frustrating – with only occasional flashes of the playwright's brilliance illuminating a long twilight of tedium.

Things probably won't have changed much for most us as we've got older. Maybe we've forced ourselves to reread the occasional play. Or perhaps we've fidgeted our way through a theatre production or film version of one of the plays.

The question, then, is whether Shakespeare is still worth the effort. Is it really worth the bother of reading plays and poetry written in obscure language that hardly anyone these days can understand straight off?

The answer is yes – and the reasons are numerous.

One reason, as your English teacher will no doubt have told you when you were studying Shakespeare in the classroom for the first time, is that 'the Bard' is now considered so important that he belongs to everybody. In common with only a few of the world's greatest artists and thinkers – Michelangelo, Beethoven, Voltaire, Picasso – Shakespeare now transcends national borders and belongs to the whole of humanity.

Wikipedia describes Shakespeare as 'the greatest writer in the English language and the world's preeminent dramatist'. Google lists 8,570,000 entries for William Shakespeare, while his works have been translated into more than 70 of the world's languages, including Latin, ancient Greek and even Klingon. A truly enormous secondary publishing industry has built up around his name and his work (this book is an example).

Familiarity with those 38 plays, 154 sonnets and other surviving works will place you very firmly in the company of the millions and millions of other people on this earth who 'get' and appreciate Shakespeare.

Another reason is that, although Shakespeare's poetry and plays were written some 400 years ago, they still resonate with remarkable insight into what it means to be human. You want to gain some insight into jealousy? Read *Othello*. You want advice on the art of seduction? *Richard III* has some great lines. You want anguish, fear, anger? Try *Hamlet*. Leontes is cruel, Lady Macbeth is ambitious, Iago is Machiavellian.

In the 400 years since Shakespeare was writing, the human condition has not changed. The same truths that held true then hold true today. In this sense, the plays and poems can be seen as a vast, still-breathing repository of human experience.

A third reason that Shakespeare still matters is the wealth and sheer unadulterated joy and inventiveness of the language he used. You only need to be aware of how many Shakespearean phrases have been passed down into modern English to know this. To take just a couple of examples, the phrase 'winter of discontent', much loved by tabloid headline writers, is a direct quote from the opening scene of *Richard III*:

> Now is the winter of our discontent
> Made glorious summer by this sun of York;
> And all the clouds that lour'd upon our house
> In the deep bosom of the ocean buried.

'Parting is such sweet sorrow', likewise, comes from Act II, scene ii of *Romeo and Juliet*:

> Good night, good night! Parting is such
> sweet sorrow,
> That I shall say good night till it be morrow.

Or how about this one: 'The course of true love never did run smooth', which comes from Act I, scene i of

*A Midsummer Night's Dream*:

> Ay me! For aught that I could ever read,
> Could ever hear by tale or history,
> The course of true love never did run smooth.

And all this really is just the tip of the iceberg. Anyone rereading the plays and the sonnets will stumble across literally hundreds of words and phrases recognisable in our own, modern-day lexicon. For this reason alone it's well worth revisiting Shakespeare.

So the short answer is that someone like Shakespeare, with so much brand recognition and continued relevance, deserves at least some working knowledge on our part. The good news is that the days of sloughing through acres and acres of set texts are over. Clearly nothing will replace a good knowledge of the original works but the following guide will provide something of a short cut to understanding why, and how, Shakespeare matters.

# OPENING LINES

Here's a selection of some of the better known opening lines from Shakespeare's plays:

> O! for a Muse of fire, that would ascend
> The brightest heaven of invention.
> *Henry V (1599)*

> When shall we three meet again?
> In thunder, lightning, or in rain?
> *Macbeth (1605)*

> Now is the winter of our discontent
> Made glorious summer by this sun of York.
> *Richard III (1592)*

> If music be the food of love, play on;
> Give me excess of it, that, surfeiting,
> The appetite may sicken, and so die.
> *Twelfth Night (1599)*

## THE SHORTEST SCENE

Antony: Set our squadrons on yon side o' the hill,
In eye of Caesar's battle, from which place
We may the number of ships behold,
and so proceed accordingly.

*Antony and Cleopatra* Act III, scene ix
Four lines; 28 words

## THE LONGEST SCENE

*Love's Labour's Lost* Act V, scene ii
920 lines, 7137 words

(I won't reproduce it here!)

## MEATIEST ROLES

Hamlet has the most lines in a single play with 1569 lines, followed by Richard III with 1151 lines. Iago has 1088 in *Othello*, while King Henry has 1031 in *Henry V*. Indeed, with starring roles in no less than three plays, Hal, later Henry V, has the largest number of lines spoken by any character across Shakespeare's plays as a whole. He appears in *Henry IV Part I* and *II* and also in *Henry V* and has 1915 lines. The character of Falstaff has the next meatiest role across more than one play with 1681 lines, followed by Richard of Gloucester (later Richard III) with 1531 lines.

Female parts, in contrast, are much shorter. Rosalind in *As You Like It* tops the table of largest speaking parts with just 685 lines, followed by Cleopatra in *Antony and Cleopatra* with 678 lines and Imogen in *Cymbeline* with 594 lines.

## FEWEST LINES

Pity the actor playing the King of France's attendant in *All's Well That Ends Well* who has just four words for the entire play: 'I shall, my liege'. The same number of words goes to the Second Pirate in *Pericles, Prince of Tyre*: 'A prize! A prize!'

For the actor who plays Taurus in *Antony and Cleopatra*, the sum of his role comes to two words: 'My Lord', while the fourth soldier in Act IV, scene ii of *Julius Caesar* has nothing to say but: 'Stand!'

But the shortest part of all goes to the second senator in *Cymbeline* Act II, scene vii who has a grand total of one word, two letters: 'Ay'.

## ANTI-SOCIAL BEHAVIOUR

Teenage anti-social behaviour is hardly new, it seems. In *The Winter's Tale*, a shepherd has it about right in Act III, scene ii where he says:

'I would there were no age between sixteen and three-and-twenty, or that youth would sleep out the rest; for there is nothing in between but getting wenches with child, wronging the ancientry, stealing, fighting.'

Nothing much changes, then.

## BINGE DRINKING

Shakespeare's plays are full of drunks and he has a lot to say on the subject of drinking to excess. In *Othello*, for example, Iago deliberately gets Cassio drunk, knowing that if he does so Cassio will be liable to get involved in a brawl and thus incur Othello's displeasure. In the event Cassio is the worst kind of drunk: quarrelsome and obnoxious, he ends up striking Roderigo and wounding Montano. In the meantime, Iago philosophises on the relative merits of the English, Danish, German and Dutch when they're drunk. He states the English are the 'most potent in potting' because an Englishman can 'drink with facility your Dane dead drunk; he sweats not to overthrow your Almaine; he gives your Hollander a vomit, 'ere the next pottle can be filled'.

In *Twelfth Night*, the appropriately named Sir Toby Belch spends much of the play reeling across the stage in a joyously drunken stupor. Feste comments that a drunken man is 'Like a drown'd man, a fool, and a madman/ One draught above heat makes him a fool, the second mads him, and a third drowns him'.

Other notable drunks are the porter in *Macbeth*, Stephano, Trinculo and Caliban in *The Tempest* – and, of course, Falstaff and his roguish companions in *Henry IV Parts I and II* and *Henry V*. But perhaps the luckiest drunk is Barnardine in *Measure for Measure*, whose execution is stayed because he is too drunk to provide consent for it.

## 'YOUR MUM'

The best example of a 'your mum'-type insult in Shakespeare is in Act IV, scene ii of *Titus Andronicus* where Aaron exclaims: 'I have done your mother.'

He means exactly what he says.

## OBSCENE GESTURES

Much has been made of the thumb-biting scene at the start of *Romeo and Juliet* where Samson, spying two followers of the house of Montague, declares: 'I will bite my thumb at them;/ Which is a disgrace to them, if they bear it.' Rude as the gesture was to an Elizabethan audience, there is at least one other very obscene gesture in Shakespeare, with a history and explanation at least as interesting as thumb biting: the Fig of Spain.

The following exchange in Act III, scene iv of *Henry V* is just one of a number of instances in which Pistol's fiery temperament finds a physical expression in the Fig of Spain:

**Fluellen:** It is well.
**Pistol:** The fig of Spain!

Here Pistol's words would have been accompanied with the actor thrusting his thumb between his middle and index fingers, the symbolism being relatively easy to work out (try it yourself).

Shakespearean audiences may or may not have known that the gesture dates back at least to ancient Rome, where it was known as the *mano fico*. Here *mano* translates as hand and *fico* as 'fig', which in itself was possibly a play on the word *fica*, a slang term referring to the female vulva.

## BEATING AROUND THE BUSH: EUPHEMISMS IN SHAKESPEARE

Euphemisms abound in Shakespeare, their difficulty and abundance providing scholars and academics more than ample scope to mine the Bard's seamier side. Here are just a few of them:

### I. Peculiar River
The phrase comes from Act I, scene ii of *Measure for Measure* where Claudio is sent to prison for 'getting Madam Julietta with child'. Mistress Overdone explains the situation to Pompey: Claudio is being punished as a result of 'Groping for trouts in a peculiar river'.

## II. Box Unseen

In Act II, scene iii of *All's Well That Ends Well*, Parolles urges Bertram to take up arms. The alternative is to wear out his 'honour' in a 'box unseen', 'spending' (i.e. ejaculating) his 'manly marrow'.

## III. Sweet Nothings

*Much Ado About Nothing* takes on an entirely different meaning if we bear in mind that 'nothing' was Elizabethan slang for a woman's unmentionables. A lot of wordplay occurs throughout Shakespeare on this theme. As an example, take Hamlet's exchange with Ophelia at the beginning of the play within a play at the start of Act III, scene ii:

**Hamlet:** Lady, shall I lie … my head upon your lap?
**Ophelia:** Ay, my lord.
**Hamlet:** Do you think I meant country matters?
**Ophelia:** I think nothing, my lord.
**Hamlet:** That's a fair thought to lie between
maids' legs.
**Ophelia:** What is, my lord?
**Hamlet:** Nothing.

## IV. Cod's Head and Salmon's Tail

In Act II, scene i of *Othello*, Iago utters the following:

> She that in wisdom never was so frail
> To change the cod's head for the salmon's tail;

Although the exact meaning of the pun has been debated, the cod's head reference is to a codpiece with the 'salmon's tail' code for female unmentionables.

## V. Velvet Leaves

In the following extract from Act I, scene iii of *Love's Labour's Lost*, the phrase 'velvet leaves' appears to be another euphemism:

> Love, whose month is ever May,
> Spied a blossom passing fair
> Playing in the wanton air
> Through the velvet leaves the wind,
> All unseen, can passage find;
> That the lover, sick to death,
> Wish himself the heaven's breath.

Here, the wind finds a way to 'triumph' by passing through the velvet leaves – something the sick lover can only aspire to.

## VI. Bird's Nest

In Act II, scene v of *Romeo and Juliet*, the nurse tells her charge that she will:

Fetch a ladder, by the which your love
Must climb a bird's nest soon when it is dark:

Scholars of sixteenth-century bawdiness relate that the bird's nest in question carries connotations of pubic hair, female genitalia, but also fertility in the form of the new life it contains.

## VII. Potato Finger

Very, very hard to believe nowadays, but in the sixteenth century the then-exotic potato was considered an aphrodisiac. This is perhaps the explanation of Falstaff's 'Let the sky rain potatoes' at his secret assignation with Mistresses Ford and Page in Act V, scene v of *The Merry Wives of Windsor*. Likewise, in Act V, scene ii of *Troilus and Cressida*, Thersites spies the heroine of the play dallying with Diomedes and exclaims: 'How the devil Luxury, with his fat rump and potato-finger, tickles these together. Fry, lechery, fry!' In this case, 'potato-finger' is a euphemism for the male member.

## HOUSEHOLD WORDS

Libraries could be filled with the famous quotes and sayings that have come down to us through Shakespeare's plays and poems. All of the following words and phrases will be familiar to the modern reader but would you have known where in the play they came from?

Though this be madness, yet there is method in 't
(Act II, scene ii)
The lady doth protest too much
(Act III, scene ii)
Brevity is the soul of wit
(Act II, scene ii)
***Hamlet***

Can I desire too much of a good thing?
(Act IV, scene i)
True is it that we have seen better days
(Act II, scene vii)
*As You Like It*

But love is blind, and lovers cannot see
(Act II, scene vi)
*The Merchant of Venice*

Why, then the world's mine oyster
(Act II, scene ii)
This is the short and the long of it
(Act II, scene ii)
I cannot tell what the dickens his name is
(Act III, scene ii)
*The Merry Wives of Windsor*

The better part of valour is discretion
(Act V, scene iv)
*King Henry IV, Part I*

He hath eaten me out of house and home
(Act II, scene i)
**King Henry IV, Part II**

I'll not budge an inch
(Act I, scene i)
**Taming of the Shrew**

But, for my own part, it was Greek to me
(Act I, scene ii)
Cry 'Havoc', and let slip the dogs of war
(Act III, scene i)
Et tu, Brute!
(Act III, scene i)
Ambition should be made of sterner stuff
(Act III, scene ii)
 **Julius Caesar**

## Gross Gourmets, Part I

In Act III, scene iv of *King Lear*, Edgar, disguised as the mad vagabond Poor Tom, describes his diet, which seems to consist largely of live amphibians, lizards, cow dung, rats, dead dogs and pond scum. Here's a list of his favourite morsels:

I.    'the swimming frog'
II.   'the toad'
III.  'the todpole' (tadpole)
IV.   ' the wall-newt' (lizard)
V.    'cow dung for sallets' (i.e. cow dung as a s ide-salad)
VI.   'old rat' (swallowed whole)
VII.  'ditch dog' (a dead dog thrown into a ditch)
VIII. 'the green mantle of the standing pool' (i.e. the scum on a stagnant pond)

## MOST INAPPROPRIATE LOVE SCENE

In Act I, scene ii of *Richard III*, Richard wins the heart of Lady Anne, whose husband, Henry VI, he has just murdered. This wooing is all the more inappropriate in that it takes place over the corpse of the dead king.

In the scene below we see Anne's initial hostility towards Richard melt in the face of some of the most eloquent and moving love poetry in the Shakespeare canon. While the audience might be amazed that Anne can so quickly forget her husband and his violent death; it can also marvel at Richard's ability to so effortlessly seduce the widow of a man he's just murdered:

**Duke of Gloucester:** Your beauty ... did haunt me in my sleep
To undertake the death of all the world,
So I might live one hour in your sweet bosom.
**Lady Anne:** If I thought that, I tell thee, homicide,
These nails should rend that beauty from my cheeks.
**Duke of Gloucester:** These eyes could never endure sweet beauty's wreck;

You should not blemish it, if I stood by:
As all the world is cheered by the sun,
So I by that; it is my day, my life.

Once Richard is left to himself, however, we see how
utterly Machiavellian he is and how this eloquence is
nothing more than camouflage for untrammelled
ambition and double-dealing:

Was ever woman in this humour woo'd?
Was ever woman in this humour won?
I'll have her; but I will not keep her long.
What! I, that kill'd her husband and his father,
To take her in her heart's extremest hate,
With curses in her mouth, tears in her eyes,
The bleeding witness of her hatred by;
Having God, her conscience, and these bars
against me,
And I nothing to back my suit at all,
But the plain devil and dissembling looks,
And yet to win her, all the world to nothing!
Ha!

# EXCLAMATIONS: 'O! O! O!'

Poignant and moving in context, some of the exclamations uttered by Shakespeare's characters can sound a bit melodramatic taken outside their setting within the play. Hence, Othello's 'O! O! O!' as he falls onto the bed next to the corpse of the wife he's just strangled may underline the intensity of his grief within the play; outside of the play's context, though, it just sounds a bit silly.

From tragedy to comedy: the Nurse's reaction on hearing of the supposed death of Juliet in Act IV, scene v of *Romeo and Juliet* is probably as heartfelt as Othello's 'O! O! O!', only potentially much funnier:

O woe! O woful, woful, woful day!
Most lamentable day, most woful day,
That ever, ever, I did yet behold!
O day! O day! O day! O hateful day!
Never was seen so black a day as this:
O woful day, O woful day!

## SHAKESPEARE IN SPACE

Twenty-four of Uranus's 27 moons are named after characters in Shakespeare's plays. Uranus' discoverer, the 18th-century English astronomer William Herschel, proposed that the planet be named 'Georgium Sidus' (George's Star) after King George III since it was the first planet discovered by an Englishman. In the event, however, the scientific community opted to continue in the classical tradition of naming planets, eventually plumping for Uranus, the ancient Greek deity of the sky, on the suggestion of German astronomer Johann Elert Bode.

In 1787, six years after announcing his discovery of Uranus, Herschel observed two moons in orbit around the planet. This time, despite continued protests from outside England, Hershel got his way when he decided to name the moons Titania and Oberon after the King and Queen of the Fairies in *A Midsummer Night's Dream*, a play by England's acknowledged national poet, Shakespeare.

When English astronomer William Lassell discovered a further two large moons in Uranus' orbit in 1851 he decided to continue with Herschel's idea of using characters from English literary works, naming the two new bodies Ariel and Umbriel from Alexander Pope's *The Rape of the Lock*. Later discoveries reverted to Shakespearean characters and now 13 of Shakespeare's plays are represented among Uranus' moons.

## I. Cordelia
The only virtuous daughter in *King Lear*.

## II. Ophelia
Polonius' daughter in *Hamlet*.

## III. Bianca
Sister of Katherine in *The Taming of the Shrew*.

## IV. Cressida
The title character in *Troilus and Cressida*.

## V. Desdemona
Othello's wife in *Othello*.

## VI. Juliet
Juliet Capulet, The title character in *Romeo and Juliet*.

## VII. Portia
Shylock's daughter in *The Merchant of Venice*.

## VIII. Rosalind
Heroine of *As You Like It*, daughter of banished Duke Senior.

## IX. Mab
Not actually a character in any play, but is referred to in *Romeo and Juliet* where Mercutio mocks Romeo for his listlessness brought on by an unrequited love for Rosaline:

> O, then, I see Queen Mab hath been with you.
> She is the fairies' midwife, and she comes
> In shape no bigger than an agate-stone
> On the fore-finger of an alderman,
> Drawn with a team of little atomies
> Athwart men's noses as they lie asleep.

*Queen Mab* is also the title of a poem by Percy Bysshe Shelley so Mab could be considered one of the moons not named after a Shakespearean character.

## X. Belinda
Another non-Shakespearean character, Belinda is a character in Alexander Pope's 18th-century mock-heroic tour de force *The Rape of the Lock*.

## XI. Perdita
Leontes' cast-away daughter in *The Winter's Tale*.

## XII. Puck
Oberon's impish servant in *A Midsummer Night's Dream*.

## XIII. Cupid
Appears in Sonnet 153 and in *Timon of Athens*.

## XIV. Miranda
Prospero's daughter in *The Tempest*.

## XV. Francisco
One of Alonso's retinue in *The Tempest*.

## XVI. Ariel
Prospero's spirit servant in *The Tempest* but also a character in Pope's *The Rape of the Lock*. Ariel, the moon,

was discovered at the same time as Umbriel so it's likely that both are named after the characters in Pope's poems rather than Shakespearean characters.

## XVII. Umbriel
From Pope's *The Rape of the Lock*.

## XVIII. Titania
Queen of the Fairies in *A Midsummer Night's Dream*.

## XIX. Oberon
King of the Fairies in *A Midsummer Night's Dream*.

## XX. Caliban
Son of the witch Sycorax and Prospero's deformed slave in *The Tempest*.

## XXI. Stephano
A drunken butler in *The Tempest*.

## XXII. Trinculo
Stephano's sidekick in *The Tempest*.

## XXIII. Sycorax
From *The Tempest*. A witch and Caliban's mother.

## XXIV. Margaret
A maid in *Much Ado About Nothing*.

## XXV. Prospero
Magician and Miranda's father in *The Tempest*.

## XXVI. Setebos
Name of the god worshipped by the witch Sycorax in *The Tempest*. Interestingly, Setebos was one of the gods worshipped by the Patagonians and has been cited as one of many clues locating the island where the action in *The Tempest* takes place somewhere off the South American mainland.

## XXVII. Ferdinand
Alonso's son in *The Tempest*.

## SHAKESPEARE ON TV

The BBC's 'Complete Dramatic Works of William Shakespeare', released between 1978 and 1985, is probably the most comprehensive small-screen rendering of the Bard's output, featuring as it does versions of every single play from the established canon.

Notable performances included Helen Mirren as Rosalind in 1979's *As You Like It*, Anthony Quayle as Falstaff in *Henry IV, Part II* (1979) and Anthony Hopkins as *Othello* (1980).

More out of the ordinary was the casting of Roger Daltrey as the Dromio twins in 1983's *The Comedy of Errors* and John Cleese as Petruchio in *The Taming of the Shrew* in 1980.

## SHOOTING SHAKESPEARE: THE BARD AT THE MOVIES

So many different versions of Shakespeare have appeared on either the small screen or in the cinema that there's easily enough material for a book in itself. *King John*, produced by Sir Herbert Beerbohm-Tree in 1899, is generally held to be the first film adaptation of a Shakespeare play. Since then there have been literally hundreds of Shakespeare movies – both faithful reproductions and versions loosely based on the original plays or using them as the starting point for new departures. Here are just a few of the acknowledged leviathans of Shakespeare on the silver screen:

## Lawrence Olivier

Quite aside from living and breathing Shakespeare in an infinite variety of stage productions, Olivier starred in and directed definitive versions of *Henry V* (1944), *Hamlet* (1948) and *Richard III* (1955). A true titan of Shakespeare at the movies.

## Orson Welles

Directed a 1948 version of *Macbeth*; directed and played *Othello* in a 1952 version of the play. Directed and played Falstaff in *Chimes at Midnight* (1967), which featured scenes from *Richard II*, *Henry IV Part I*, *Henry IV Part II*, *Henry V* and *The Merry Wives of Windsor*.

## Akira Kurosawa

Best known for his virtuoso retellings in Japanese of the best-known tragedies. *The Bad Sleep Well* (*Warui Yatsu Hodo Yoku Nemuru*, 1960) is a quirky retelling of *Hamlet*, while *Ran* (1985) is a very loose adaptation of *King Lear*. *The Throne of Blood* (*Kumonosu-jo*), also known as *The Castle of the Spider's Web*, 1957, meanwhile, is generally acknowledged as the most accomplished foreign language version of *Macbeth*.

## Roman Polanski

Polanski's 1971 gore-fest adaptation of *Macbeth* is notable not just for a nude sleep-walking scene featuring a nubile Francesca Annis but also for its ultra-violent depiction of Duncan's assassination and the mountain of folklore that's built up around Polanski's association with the Manson murders and its influence on the film.

## Franco Zeffirelli

Another director whose name has become synonymous with classic on-screen takes of Shakespeare. His 1966 version of *The Taming of the Shrew* in which Elizabeth Taylor and Richard Burton played Katherine and

Petruchios, was followed up a year later with a box-office smash retelling of *Romeo and Juliet*, with Olivia Hussey and Leonard Whiting as Romeo and Juliet, Michael York as Tybalt, John McEnery as Mercutio, and Pat Heywood as the Nurse. A more recent Zeffirelli foray into the Shakespeare canon was 1990's production of *Hamlet* that boasted Mel Gibson in the lead role and Glenn Close as Gertrude.

## Kenneth Branagh

Branagh's Shakespeare credentials go far beyond any single acting or directorial role: he has been credited with reviving interest in Shakespeare as a cinematic experience.

In *Henry V* (director, 1989), he played Hal, alongside Ian Holm as Fluellen, Brian Blessed as Exeter and Emma Thompson as Katherine.

In an all-star version of *Much Ado About Nothing* (director, 1993) he played Benedick, with Emma Thompson as Beatrice, Denzel Washington as Don Pedro, Robert Sean Leonard as Claudio, Kate Beckinsale as Hero, Michael Keaton as Dogberry and Keanu Reeves as Don John.

*Othello* (1995) saw Branagh relinquish directorial control in favour of a masterful performance as an ingratiating and thoroughly untrustworthy Iago.

In 1996's four-hour *Hamlet*, Branagh as director is credited with the only totally unexpurgated version of the play on film. A loss of form in 2000's widely panned musical rendition of *Love's Labour's Lost* was followed in 2006 with *As You Like It* with Kevin Kline as Jaques and Alfred Molina as Touchstone.

## OTHER NOTEWORTHY SHAKESPEAREANS

**Douglas Fairbanks**
Petruchio, *The Taming of the Shrew* (1929)

**James Cagney**
Bottom, *A Midsummer Night's Dream* (1935)

**Mickey Rooney**
Puck, *A Midsummer Night's Dream* (1935)

**Charlton Heston**
Mark Antony, *Julius Caesar* (1949)

Mark Antony, *Julius Caesar* (1970)
Director, Antony, *Antony and Cleopatra* (1972)

**Marlon Brando**
Mark Antony, *Julius Caesar* (1953)

**John Gielgud**
Cassius, *Julius Caesar* (USA, 1953)
Clarence, *Richard III* (UK, 1955)
Henry IV, *Chimes at Midnight* (1967)
Caesar, *Julius Caesar* (USA, 1970)
Prospero, *Prospero's Books* (adaptation of *The Tempest* 1991)

**Leslie Nielsen**
The Captain, *Forbidden Planet* (1956)

**Kenneth Williams**
Caesar, *Carry On Cleo* (very loose adaptation of *Antony and Cleopatra* and *Julius Caesar*, 1965)

**Diana Rigg**
Edwina Lionheart, *Theatre of Blood* (1973)

**Derek Jarman**
Director, *The Tempest* (1979)

**Toyah Willcox**
Miranda, *The Tempest* (1979)

**Molly Ringwald**
Miranda, *Tempest* (1982)
Cordelia, *King Lear* (Jean-Luc Godard directed science fiction adaptation of the play, 1987)

**Ben Kingsley**
Feste, *Twelfth Night* (1996)

**Helena Bonham Carter**
Olivia, *Twelfth Night* (1996)

**Imogen Stubbs**
Viola, *Twelfth Night* (1996)

**Richard E. Grant**
Sir Andrew Aguecheek, *Twelfth Night* (1996)

## Anthony Hopkins
Titus Andronicus, *Titus Andronicus* (1999)

## Heath Ledger
Patrick Verona, *10 Things I Hate about You*
(A loose adaptation of *The Taming of the Shrew*, 1999)

## Michelle Pfeiffer
Titania, *A Midsummer Night's Dream* (1999)

## Julia Stiles
Kat, *10 Things I Hate About You*
*Desi, O* (modern adaptation of *Othello*, 2001)

## Kevin Kline
Bottom, *A Midsummer Night's Dream* (1999)
Jaques, *As You Like It* (2006)

## Al Pacino
Shylock, *The Merchant of Venice* (2004)

## Jeremy Irons
Antonio, *The Merchant of Venice* (2004)

## SCIENCE FICTION

For some reason, science fiction writers for television and film have a bit of a thing for using quotes from Shakespeare for the titles of their episodes. *Star Trek* writers are probably the worst culprits with episodes from both the original series and later spin-offs borrowing Shakepearisms for their titles.

*Hamlet* seems to have had the most profound influence on *Star Trek* writers with at least four borrowings from the play used as titles, including 'The Undiscovered Country' for one of the *Star Trek* movies (Act III, scene i); 'The Conscience of the King' for an episode from the original series (Act II, scene ii); 'Thine Own Self' for a *Star Trek: The Next Generation* episode (Act I, scene iii) and 'Mortal Coil' for a *Star Trek: Voyager* episode (Act III, scene i).

'The Dogs of War', the title of a *Star Trek: Deep Space Nine* episode, comes from Act III, scene i of *Julius Caesar*, while 'Dagger of the Mind' and 'All Our Yesterdays' for episodes of the original *Star Trek* come from *Macbeth* Act II, scene i and Act V, scene v respectively. 'Once More Unto the Breach', for a *Star Trek:*

*Deep Space Nine* episode comes from *Henry V*, Act III, scene I, while *King Lear* (Act I, scene iv) is the inspiration for the 'How Sharper Than A Serpent's Tooth' episode from the animated *Star Trek* series ('How sharper than a serpent's tooth it is to have a thankless child').

Finally, the title for the *Star Trek* episode entitled 'By Any Other Name' takes its inspiration from the famous balcony scene in Act II, scene ii of *Romeo and Juliet* where Juliet asks: 'What's in a name? That which we call a rose / By any other name would still smell as sweet.'

Cult sci-fi series *Babylon 5* is another Shakespeare sci-fi culprit with an episode titled 'The Paragon of Animals' (from *Hamlet*, Act II, scene ii) and another entitled 'The Quality of Mercy' (from *The Merchant of Venice*, Act II, scene ii).

*Buffy*, of vampire-slaying fame, has one of the books in the spin-off novels adapted from the television series using a Shakespeare quote for its title: 'The Evil that Men Do'. The original is from the famous 'Friends, Romans, countrymen' speech in Act III, scene ii of *Julius Caesar* where Mark Antony gives the funeral oration over the body of the dead emperor:

I come to bury Caesar, not to praise him.
The evil that men do lives after them,
The good is oft interred with their bones.

*Forbidden Planet*, meanwhile, is a 1956 sci-fi movie classic and is loosely based on *The Tempest*. In the film, Robby the Robot can be read either as a hi-tech re-rendering of Caliban or as an updated version of Ariel, while the Krell resemble Sycorax.

Finally, no discussion of Shakespeare in science fiction would be complete without mention of *Dr Who*, but this deserves a section to itself.

## SHAKESPEARE AND THE TIMELORD

*Dr Who* aficionados know that the Timelord's contact with the Bard goes way beyond 'The Shakespeare Code', the episode of the revived science fiction series first aired on the BBC in 2007.

In 'The Chase', from 1965, the first Doctor, played by William Hartnell, and his companions gather round the

Time Space Visualiser, a device that allows them to watch any event from any time and any place in history. Barbara Wright, played by Jacqueline Hill, chooses to watch an encounter between Elizabeth I and Shakespeare. They thus witness Elizabeth I providing the inspiration for *The Merry Wives of Windsor* and *Hamlet*.

In 'The Planet of Evil', first aired in 1975, Tom Baker, playing the fourth Doctor, quotes from *Hamlet* and from *Romeo and Juliet*. He claims to have known the playwright before the start of his literary career. The plot for 'The Planet of Evil' takes its cue from *Forbidden Planet*, which in turn is partly based on *The Tempest*.

In 1979's 'City of Death', Tom Baker claims he helped Shakespeare write *Hamlet* after the Bard injured his wrist writing sonnets.

In 'The Mark of the Rani', first aired in 1985, the sixth Doctor, played by Colin Baker, notes that he would like to meet up with Shakespeare again at some point.

In 2005's 'The Christmas Invasion', David Tennant, in the role of the tenth Doctor, foils an invasion of Earth by the Sycorax. As in so many science fiction borrowings from Shakespeare, *The Tempest* is again the inspiration here: Sycorax the witch is Caliban's mother in the play.

The Doctor is also fond of quoting Shakespeare. In 'The Image of the Fendahl', first aired in 1977, Tom Baker addresses a skull with the phrase 'Alas, Poor Skull!' In 'Castrovalva', first aired in 1982, Peter Davison, the fifth Doctor, states he will 'Go softly on!' Likewise, in 1985's 'The Two Doctors', Colin Baker as the sixth Doctor says, 'Good-night, sweet prince,' to a dying colleague.

## SHAKESPEARE AND THE TIMELORD: 'THE SHAKESPEARE CODE'

'The Shakespeare Code' is a 2007 *Dr Who* episode that borrows heavily from Shakespeare for its storyline. Here, the tenth Doctor, played by David Tennant, is accompanied by Martha Jones on her first trip in the Tardis as the Doctor's assistant. Their destination is Elizabethan England – and, naturally, on arrival one of the first things they do is to bump into Shakespeare, who is busily putting the finishing touches to a new play, '*Love's Labour Won*'. Unbeknownst to them, however, the Carrionites, evil, witch-like aliens, aim to destroy the world by inserting a magical code into the closing words of the play. As you'd expect, the Doctor saves the day but not before much fun has been had by the writers of the episode with the concept of the Doctor interacting with the playwright. Among other things, the Doctor is credited with the authorship of Sonnet 18 and inspires Shakespeare with the phrases 'All the world's a stage', 'The play's the thing', 'Once more unto the breach' and 'To be or not to be', all of which, of course, come famously from the Shakespeare canon.

Interestingly, the three Carrionites, who appear to be modelled on the Three Weird Sisters from *Macbeth*, use trochaic tetrameter and rhyming couplets for their spells as do the witches in the original play.

## *SOUTH PARK*: 'SCOTT TENORMAN MUST DIE'

Episode 69 of the classic adult comedy animation series is loosely based on the plot of *Titus Andronicus*, Shakespeare's bloodiest play and a classic of the

Elizabethan revenge-tragedy genre.

In the *South Park* version, Cartman cooks up an elaborate revenge on 15-year-old schoolboy Scott Tenorman, who among other things has tricked him into paying $10 for a handful of his pubic hair. Cartman's revenge revolves around a wiener-eating pony, the band Radiohead and a chilli cook-off.

As in *Titus Andronicus*, the culmination of the revenge theme is a horrific, unintentional act of cannibalism involving a close family member. In *Titus Andronicus*, Titus takes his revenge on the Empress Tamora by killing then cooking her sons Demetrius and Chiron and serving them up to her in a pie for dinner.

In the *South Park* episode, Cartman uses the hacked-up remains of Tenorman's parents as the ingredients for his chilli in the cook-off. On discovering this, Tenorman bursts into tears, prompting his favourite band, Radiohead, who have just appeared, to label him 'deeply uncool'. Cartman then licks Tenorman's tears and utters the immortal, almost Shakespearean lines:

'Ohhh, the tears of unfathomable sadness, mmm, yummy … yummy!'

And:

'I made you eat your parents! I made you eat your parents!'

The episode was voted the most outrageous *South Park* episode by Comedy Central, the most popular episode by TV.com and the most rated episode by the Internet Movie Database.

## *BLACKADDER* AND THE BARD

Classic BBC comedy series *Blackadder* paid its own unique homage to Shakespeare in 1999's *Blackadder Back & Forth*, in which Baldrick invents a time machine allowing Edmund to travel back to Elizabethan England. Bumping into Shakespeare in a corridor, Edmund first asks for his autograph then knocks him down with a single punch. He tells a nonplussed Shakespeare that the punch is on behalf every schoolboy and schoolgirl for the next four hundred years:

Have you any idea how much suffering you are going to cause? Hours spent at school desks trying to find one joke in *A Midsummer Night's Dream*? Years wearing stupid tights in school plays and saying things like 'What ho, my lord' and 'Oh, look, here comes Othello, talking total crap as usual'.

Later in the episode, Edmund returns to England to find things have been put out of joint by his escapades: Shakespeare is now only known as the inventor of the biro. He has no choice but to go back in time once again and set things straight. This time, when he encounters Shakespeare, the following exchange takes place:

**Blackadder:** I'm a very big fan, Bill.
**Shakespeare:** Thank you.
**Blackadder:** Keep up the good work. *King Lear* – very funny.

## THE SIMPSONS

In 'Tales from the Public Domain', *The Simpsons* pay homage to *Hamlet* with Bart in the lead role. Moe plays Claudius, who marries Marge (as Gertrude) after poisoning King Hamlet (Homer). Homer returns as a ghost to incite Bart to revenge, while the famous play-within-a-play scene is helped along with the aid of Krusty the Clown. Bart (as Hamlet) accidentally kills Polonius (Chief Wiggum) after which his son, Laertes (Ralph), challenges him to a duel.

True to the original, the story ends with a death-fest. Ralph, attempting a practice stab in his duel with Bart kills himself, after which Bart kills Claudius. Carl and Lenny (playing Rosencarl and Guildenlenny) kill each other with poisoned high fives while Bart dies after slipping on some blood. Marge kills herself with a mace after seeing how much mess there is to tidy up.

A second *Simpsons* reference to Shakespeare came in Season 15 episode 'Co-Dependent's Day'. In the episode Moe slips up by giving away a priceless 1886 bottle of Chateau Latour. On discovering his mistake he bursts into tears – using a valuable original manuscript of

Shakespeare's *The Two Noble Kinsmen* to dry his tears. It's possibly the widest airing the play has ever had: it's the only one of Shakespeare's plays that has never been adapted for television or the movies.

## INFANTICIDE

Macduff's young son is killed in the fourth act of *Macbeth* but not before he utters a classic Shakespearean insult after hearing his father accused of treason: 'Thou liest, thou shag-haired villain!' The murderer's response is similarly ripe: 'What, you egg, / Young fry of treachery!' Whether the punning on fry and egg was intentional is a different matter.

## OBESITY

In *The Comedy of Errors,* Dromio of Syracuse discovers that Nell, an overweight kitchen-maid, has been lusting after him. He describes her as 'spherical, like a globe', adding: 'I could find out countries in her.' He says that Ireland is 'in her buttocks' and that he 'found it out by the bogs'.

In *Henry IV, Part I* Mistress Quickly describes how Falstaff has eaten her 'out of house and home' and how he has: 'put all my substance into that fat belly of his'. Later in the same play Hal describes Falstaff as a 'fat villain', while Doll Tearsheet likens him to 'a hulk … stuffed in the hold'.

Dr Johnson probably has the best line when describing Falstaff's rotundity, however. He called him a 'swollen excrescence of a man'.

# POTTED PLOTS

In which I reduce some of Shakespeare's masterpieces to a paragraph ...

## MACBETH

Witches entertain themselves by making up cod prophesy of kingship for Macbeth, a vicious Scottish warlord. Macbeth foolishly tells trophy wife about possible kingship promotion; wife mocks him; says he's weak when he says he'd rather 'Do the Right Thing'. Macbeth can't handle the mockery; murders current king; is crowned. Doesn't trust best mate so has him assassinated; sees best mate's ghost; trophy wife goes mad, commits suicide; more murders, loads of blood, gore and witches; Edward the Confessor saves the day. Macbeth dies.

## KING LEAR

Old King disinherits virtuous daughter while giving up his kingdom to her two evil siblings; gets upset when said siblings stint on hospitality to their aged parent, goes mad, rips off clothes, runs amok on heathland during a thunderstorm, howls at moon. Meanwhile, Duke of Gloucester has his eyes poked out by old king's evil son-in-law. Virtuous daughter raises army; baddies get their comeuppance through stabbings, poison and sword fights but not before virtuous daughter (hanged) and king (broken heart; old age) both die.

## HAMLET

Hamlet, Prince of Denmark, communes with the ghost of his father, who unbeknownst to everyone was murdered by Hamlet's uncle – now king – who is now married to his mother, the queen. Understandably upset, the Prince plots his revenge – but feigns madness to deflect suspicion. Play climaxes with the death of the queen (poisoned chalice), the death of Ophelia's brother Laertes (stabbed by a poisoned rapier), the death of the king (stabbed by the poisoned rapier, forced to drink from the poisoned chalice) and the death of Hamlet (stabbed by the poisoned rapier, chooses to drink from the poisoned chalice). Horatio wants to die too; Hamlet won't let him. Fortinbras becomes king.

## HENRY IV PART II

Play opens with rumours of the death of Henry IV and Hal, his lackadaisical son (later of 'Once more unto the breach' and 'St Crispin's Day' fame). Rumour is wrong: the king returns to dreams of crusading in Jerusalem; Hal to the company of rotund ne'er-do-well Falstaff. Much Shakespearean innuendo and practical joking. This interrupted by the revolt of the Archbishop of York and the Duke of Northumberland. The king summons Hal, leaving Falstaff to travel to Gloucestershire to recruit soldiers to the king's cause. Further comic interludes. Yorkist army runs away after being foiled by cunning plan carried out by John, Hal's cold-hearted-but-dull younger brother. Hal returns to London, snatches crown off still-undead father, apologises, becomes king then snubs Falstaff when he next bumps into him. Falstaff sent to prison by his arch enemy, the Lord Chief Justice.

## SHAKESPEAREAN FILTH: MORE EUPHEMISMS

### I. Dearest bodily part

This comes from Act I, scene iv of *Cymbeline*, where the evil Iachimo lays a bet with Posthumus that he will 'enjoy ... the dearest bodily part of [his] mistress', Imogen.

### II. Flashing fire

In Act II, scene i of *Henry V*, Pistol's fighting talk contains the following: 'Pistol's cock is up,/ And flashing fire will follow'. This sort of euphemistic wordplay on Pistol's name occurs throughout parts I and II of *Henry IV* and in *Henry V*.

### III. Hanging bugles in an invisible baldric

To hang one's bugle in an invisible baldric is one of the more complicated of Shakespeare's innuendos and much scholarly ink has been spilled debating the meaning of this particular phrase as a result. It appears in Benedick's speech in Act I, scene i of *Much Ado About Nothing* in which he vows to remain a bachelor:

> That a woman conceived me, I thank her; that she brought me up, I likewise give her most humble thanks: but that I will have a recheat winded in my forehead, or hang my bugle in an invisible baldrick, all women shall pardon me.

Here, a 'recheat' is a call from a hunting horn (for some reason, horns of any kind had an indelible association with sex in the Elizabethan mindset) – to have it winded on your forehead would be to grow cuckold's horns; i.e. to have an unfaithful wife or lover. The bugle could be a euphemism for the male member, while a baldric is a belt for hanging a bugle, which here can be taken to be that hardy perennial of Elizabethan fashion, the codpiece. One reading then is that Benedick refuses to be cowed into making his manhood (i.e. bugle) inconspicuous by hiding it in an unostentatious cod-piece (baldric).

## IV. Feeling horny

The Forester's song in Act IV, scene ii of *As You Like It* contains the following lines:

> Take thou no scorn to wear the horn ...
> Thy father's father wore it; And thy father bore it.
> The horn, the horn, the lusty horn,
> Is not a thing to laugh to scorn.

Here the reference is both to the cuckold's horns but also to male genitalia.

## V. Three-inch fool

Size matters, at least if Grumio is to be believed in Act IV, scene i of *The Taming of the Shrew*. Here, he responds to Curtis' 'Away, you three-inch fool!' with the following (note, yet again, the reference to cuckold's horns):

Am I but three inches? Why, thy horn is a foot, and so long am I at the least.

## VI. Pizzle

Falstaff in *Henry IV, Part I*, on learning of the plot by Hal and Poins to rob him, utters some splendidly filthy invective with more than one euphemistic reference to male genitalia:

> 'Sblood, you starveling, you elf-skin, you dried
> neat's tongue, you bull's pizzle, you stock-fish!
> O for breath to utter what is like thee! you
> tailor's-yard, you sheath, you bowcase; you vile
> standing-tuck –

# LITERARY CROSS-FERTILISATIONS:
## NOVELS AND SHORT STORIES

**I.** *Brave New World*, title of Aldous Huxley's dystopian novel. Original lines from *The Tempest* (1607), Act V, scene i. Miranda, seeing other people aside from herself and her father for the first time, exclaims:

How many goodly people are there here!
How beauteous mankind is! O! brave new world,
That has such people in't.

**II.** *Under the Greenwood Tree*, used by Thomas Hardy as the title of his 1872 novel. Original lines come from a song in *As You Like It* (1599) Act II, scene v:

Under the Greenwood tree
Who loves to lie with me,

And turn his merry note
Unto the sweet bird's throat,
Come hither, come hither, come hither:
Here shall he see
No enemy
But winter and rough weather.

**III.** *The Darling Buds of May*, title of HE Bates' novels and short stories about the Larkin family. Original lines from Sonnet 18:

Shall I compare thee to a summer's day?
Thou art more lovely and more temperate:
Rough winds do shake the darling buds of May,
And summer's lease doth have all too short a date.

**IV.** *The Winter of our Discontent*, title of John Steinbeck's last major novel. Published in 1961, it was panned by critics. Original lines from *Richard III*, Act I, scene i:

Now is the winter of our discontent
Made glorious summer by this sun of York;

**V.** *Something Wicked this Way Comes*, a 1962 fantasy horror by Ray Bradbury. The original is spoken by one of the witches in *Macbeth* Act IV; scene i just ahead of Macbeth's arrival in the cavern:

> By the pricking of my thumbs / Something wicked this way comes.

The scene confirms *Macbeth* in his move to the Dark Side.

**VI.** *Mortal Coils*, by Aldous Huxley, is the name given to a 1922 collection of short stories. The original is from the 'To be, or not to be' speech in *Hamlet* Act III, scene i where Hamlet is pondering the afterlife:

> For in that sleep of death what dreams may come
> When we have shuffled off this mortal coil,

**VII.** *Time Out of Joint*, Phillip K Dick's 1959 novel was the inspiration for hit 1998 movie *The Truman Show*. The original lines are from Act I, scene v of *Hamlet* after the protagonist has learned from the ghost of his father's murder. Here, the film mirrors the play and

Dick's 1959 novel in that a superficially untroubled world conceals uncomfortable and only guessed at truths that the protagonist has to uncover to regain his freedom. In Hamlet's words:

The time is out of joint. O cursed spite
That ever I was born to set it right!

VIII. *Time Must have a Stop* (1944) another Shakespearism for a title of one of Huxley's novels. This time the line is from *Henry IV, Part I* and is from Hotspur's splendid dying speech after being wounded by Hal on the battlefield:

O, Harry, thou hast robb'd me of my youth!
I better brook the loss of brittle life
Than those proud titles thou hast won of me;
They wound my thoughts worse than sword my
flesh:
But thought's the slave of life, and life time's fool;
And time, that takes survey of all the world,
Must have a stop.

**IX.** ***The Glimpses of the Moon***, Edith Wharton's 1922 follow-on from the Pulitzer Prize-winning *Age of Innocence*. Original lines from *Hamlet* Act I, scene iv, in which the Prince confronts the ghost of his father asking him why he has returned to haunt him:

> What may this mean
> That thou, dead corse, again in complete steel,
> Revisits thus the glimpses of the moon,
> Making night hideous,

**X.** ***Tomorrow and Tomorrow and Tomorrow:*** the original for Kurt Vonnegut's short story comes from Act V scene v of *Macbeth* in which the king takes time out from defying the approaching armies of Malcolm to respond to the news that his wife is dead:

> She should have died hereafter;
> There would have been a time for such a word.
> To-morrow, and to-morrow, and to-morrow,
> Creeps in this petty pace from day to day
> To the last syllable of recorded time,

And all our yesterdays have lighted fools
The way to dusty death.

## MAGICIANS: GLENDOWER AND PROSPERO

A belief in magic in Shakespeare goes beyond the three witches in *Macbeth*. In Glendower in *Henry IV, Part I* and Prospero in *The Tempest*, the audience gets a glimpse of two magicians who have a deep faith in their ability to fashion the world according to their desires through the power of magic.

Glendower bears witness to his own magical powers. He says his birth was marked by 'fiery shapes' in the heavens and earthquakes and that he can 'call spirits from the vasty deep' and 'command the devil'. Unfortunately, his knowledge of 'deep experiments' does nothing to impress fellow rebel Hotspur, who evidently holds such 'skimble-skamble stuff' in poor regard. He describes how Glendower held him for nine hours 'in reckoning up the several devils' names/ That were his lackeys'. He adds:

Sometimes he angers me
With telling of the Moldwarp [i.e. mole] and the ant,
Of the dreamer Merlin and his prophesies,
And of a dragon and a finless fish.

For all Glendower's bombast, Prospero in *The Tempest* is an altogether more successful and convincing magician. It is left to Caliban to describe how Prospero's spirits appear to torment him 'sometimes like apes', 'then like hedgehogs', and then like adders to 'hiss [him] into madness'.

## GHOSTLY PROTOCOLS

In the opening scene of *Hamlet*, Shakespeare provides his audience with a perfectly practical 'how to' guide for confronting ghosts. In the play, Francesco, Barnado, Marcellus and Horatio are discussing an apparition that's been stalking the battlements of Elsinore castle for the past couple of days when suddenly the ghost reappears. Shakespeare's stage directions and the reactions of the characters reveal much about 17th-century protocols for dealing with ghosts – protocols of which a modern-day audience may well be blissfully and dangerously unaware:

## I. Always address ghosts in Latin

This is the reason Horatio – described as 'a scholar' by his companions – is urged to be the one to talk to the ghost. The tradition that ghosts and representatives of the spirit world are more likely to understand Latin persists to this day: Exorcisms, and the Black Mass, for example, are in Latin and the association of Latin with magic and the spirit world also still exists: think Harry Potter's *expeliamus*, for example. In the event, theatrical convention requires Horatio to speak to the ghost in English in the play (otherwise the audience wouldn't have understood him) – but the point about Latin stands. In Hamlet's first meeting with the ghost in Act I, scene v, for example, he exclaims: *'Hic et ubique'* (here and everywhere) – when urged by the disembodied voice of the ghost to swear to revenge his murder.

## II. Ghosts will not speak unless spoken to

This is evident in *Hamlet*, where Marcellus urges Horatio to 'speak to it' [the ghost] and again later in the same scene where Horatio says:

> Stay, illusion,
> If thou hast any sound or use of voice,
> Speak to me.

In the event, only the dead king's son has the power to make the ghost speak and it is not until the fifth scene of Act I with Hamlet's 'Speak. I'll go no further' that the ghost utters its first sound: 'Mark me'.

## III. On hearing a cock crow, ghosts will be forced to return to the underworld

This is exactly what happens to the ghost in the first scene of *Hamlet*. In Marcellus' words: 'It faded on the crowing of the cock'. This is also the basis for the belief as expressed by Marcellus in the same scene that on Christmas Eve the cock crows all night so that 'no spirit dare stir abroad', preventing any evil from happening ahead of Christmas Day itself. As a result:

The nights are wholesome; then no planets strike;
No fairy takes; nor witch hath power to charm.
So hallowed and so gracious is that time.

Presumably, the reasoning here is that the cock's crow heralds the breaking of the dawn and ghosts – only being permitted by the guardians of the spirit world to walk at night – are fooled into thinking that dawn approaches with the crowing of the cock and so disappear.

## IV. Try to find out why the ghost has appeared

In Horatio's attempted interrogation of the ghost in the first scene of *Hamlet*, he runs through the most typical explanations for ghostly apparitions:

1) The ghost needs something to be done for it, such as the burial of its body ('If there be any good thing to be done/ that may to thee do ease and grace to me,/ Speak to me.')
2) The ghost is an omen ('If thou art privy to thy country's fate,/ Which happily foreknowing may avoid./ O, speak!')

3) The ghost has buried treasure on its conscience ('If thou hast uphoarded in thy life / Extorted treasure in the womb of the earth, / For which, they say, you spirits oft walk in death, / Speak of it')

Unfortunately, the cock crows and the ghost disappears before Horatio has a chance to reach a fourth possible explanation for its appearance – to demand revenge for its murder.

## MORE GHOSTS AND GHOULS

Ghostly apparitions play a large part in Shakespeare. We've already seen the methods Hamlet and Horatio have of dealing with the appearance of Hamlet's murdered father – but there are other ghosts that appear in the plays. Here are a few of them:

### I. Banquo
In *Macbeth*, the murderous king is confronted by the ghost of Banquo, whom he has ordered to be assassinat-

ed along with his son Fleance. In the event, Fleance escapes, but the murderers succeed in cutting Banquo's throat and leave him lying in a ditch 'with twenty trenched gashes on his head'. Macbeth learns of this as he is hosting a banquet, but his satisfaction at the plot's success is cut short by the appearance of Banquo's blood-drenched ghost, who enters the room and sits at the king's place at the table. Unlike Old Hamlet's ghost, Banquo is silent and only Macbeth is able to see him. The king's first response on seeing the ghost paints its own grisly picture though: 'Thou canst not say I did it; never shake/ Thy gory locks at me.'

## II. Julius Caesar

In *Hamlet*, Horatio relates how ahead of the assassination of Julius Caesar, 'The graves stood tenantless and the sheeted dead/ Did squeak and gibber in the Roman streets'. In Shakespeare's retelling of the Emperor's murder the ghosts also appear after the murder. Here, as in *Macbeth*, it is a guilty conscience that prompts the appearance of a wronged spirit: Brutus is confronted by the ghost of the Caesar he helped to kill. As in *Hamlet*, Brutus must prompt the spirit to explain its presence:

'Art thou some god, some angel, or some devil,/ That makest my blood cold and my hair to stare?/ Speak to me what thou art.' Caesar then tells him he will see him again on the battlefield and disappears.

### III. Richard III

When it comes to guilty consciences and ghostly apparitions, *Richard III* takes some beating. In Act V, scene iii of the play, on the eve of the Battle of Bosworth, the king is confronted by the ghosts of a full cast of 11 characters in whose deaths he has played a part. They are: Prince Edward, Henry VI, George, Duke of Clarence, Lord Rivers, Earl Grey, Sir Thomas Vaughan, Lord Hastings, the young princes, The Duke of Buckingham and Lady Anne. Each of them curses the king, exhorting him to 'despair, and die!'

## What's Eating Shylock?

Of all of Shakespeare's characters Shylock has to win first prize for avarice – and this vice can be considered to be one of the driving forces for his general nastiness throughout the play. When his daughter elopes with Lorenzo – carrying off his stock of gold and jewellery in the process – his first concern is not for the loss of his daughter's love but for the loss of his material wealth. His mixed-up priorities find expression with the following: 'I would my daughter were dead at my foot, and the ducats in her coffin!' Earlier in the play, Salanio mocks Shylock's confused reaction to the loss of his daughter and his gold:

The dog Jew did utter in the streets:
'My daughter! - O my ducats! - O my daughter!
Fled with a Christian! - O my Christian ducats! -
Justice! The law! My ducats, and my daughter!

# SOUND FAMILIAR? MORE HOUSEHOLD PHRASES

There's daggers in men's smiles (Act II, scene iii)
What's done is done (Act III, scene ii)
All the perfumes of Arabia will not sweeten this
little hand (Act V, scene i)
*Macbeth*

How sharper than a serpent's tooth it is to have a
thankless child! (Act I, scene iv)
Nothing will come of nothing (Act I, scene i)
Have more than thou showest, speak less than thou
knowest, lend less than thou owest (Act I, scene iv)
*King Lear*

'Tis neither here nor there (Act IV, scene iii)
I will wear my heart upon my sleeve for daws to
peck at (Act I, scene i)
*Othello*

The game is up (Act III, scene iii)
I have not slept one wink (Act III, scene iii)
*Cymbeline*

We are such stuff as dreams are made on, rounded
with a little sleep (Act IV, scene i)
**The Tempest**

The course of true love never did run smooth
(Act I, scene i)
**A Midsummer Night's Dream**

Out of the jaws of death (Act III, scene iv)
**The Taming of the Shrew**

## THE ACT OF DARKNESS: MORE SEX IN SHAKESPEARE

There is a lot of sex in Shakespeare, though not always
necessarily visible to the naked eye. Quite often,
Shakespeare's characters use animal imagery to empha-
sise a sense of disgust at the sexual act. In *Cymbeline*, for
example, Posthumus Leonatus describes his belief that
Iachimo has seduced his wife, Imogen, and:

Like a full-acorn'd boar, a German one,
Cried 'O!' and mounted;

In *Othello*, Iago describes sex as 'making the beast with two backs'. Later in the play, Othello relates how Cassio and Desdemona 'hath the act of shame/ A thousand times committed'.

In *King Lear*, Edgar, disguised as Poor Tom, describes how in a previous life he had 'served the lust of [his] mistress' heart and did the act of darkness with her'.

More comically, Falstaff, disguised as Herne the Hunter in *The Merry Wives of Windsor*, describes how love 'in some respects, makes a beast a man, in some other, a man a beast'. Which side of the fence Falstaff falls on when it comes to loving becomes clear with the following:

For me, I am here a
Windsor stag; and the fattest, I think, i' the
forest. Send me a cool rut-time, Jove, or who can
blame me to piss my tallow?

## WORST BODY ODOUR

Caliban in *The Tempest* and Cloten in *Cymbeline* vie for the honour of being the smelliest character in Shakespeare.

In *Cymbeline*, Cloten exerts himself in a sword fight, making him 'reek like a sacrifice'.

In *The Tempest*, Trinculo, finding Caliban, says he 'smells like a fish; a very ancient and fish-like smell; a kind of not-of-the-newest poor-john: a strange fish'.

## DISGUISES

So many of Shakespeare's plots are constructed around the use of disguises to conceal identity that it's hard to know where to begin.

In *Measure for Measure*, the Duke disguises himself as a friar so he can spy on Angelo. He only reveals his true identity after the full extent of Angelo's skulduggery has been revealed.

In *Cymbeline*, Iachimo dresses up in Leonatus' clothes, making Imogen believe her husband has been killed when she finds his decapitated body. Later in the same play, Leonatus disguises himself as a Roman soldier in the hope of dying on the battlefield.

In *Henry IV, Part I*, Hal and Poins disguise themselves in buckram (i.e. coarse linen) suits to rob Falstaff.

In *The Merry Wives of Windsor* it's Falstaff who turns up in disguise: in this instance Mistress Ford and Mistress Page gull him into first dressing up as a fat witch and then as Herne the Hunter. His reward in both cases is a sound beating.

In *Henry V*, the king conceals his identity ahead of the Battle of Agincourt, fooling Pistol into thinking he is Harry Le Roy, an infantryman and 'a gentleman of a company'.

But perhaps the most interesting disguise of all though is that of Poor Tom in *King Lear*. Here Edgar, who has been wrongly accused of plotting against his father, disguises himself to 'take the basest and most poorest shape / that ever penury ... / Brought near to beast'. Transformed as 'Poor Tom' he spends much of Acts II, III and IV masquerading as a mad beggar, and talking gibberish to imaginary demons. He takes his cue from the 'Bedlam beggars' he has seen who put 'pins, wooden pricks, nails, sprigs of rosemary' in their 'numbed and mortified bare arms' with the object of eliciting sympathy and charity from passers-by. Actors playing Edgar have been known to take these stage directions literally – making for a painfully realistic interpretation of the Poor Tom character.

## GENDER BENDERS

Gender-play figures large in Shakespeare. This is perhaps unsurprising given the ban on actresses on the Elizabethan stage: the inversion of traditional male and female roles was almost a given within the notoriously racy confines of the playhouse.

In *As You Like It*, Rosalind disguises herself as 'Ganymede', while her companion Celia takes on the disguise of 'Aliena'. As an example of gender confusion in Shakespeare, Ganymede's mock wooing by her pretended suitor Orlando at the end of Act IV is hard to beat: theatregoers would have been presented with a boy actor pretending to be a woman, pretending to be a man, pretending to be a woman, being wooed by a man superficially unaware that the boy he is pretending to woo is a boy pretending to be a woman pretending to be a man pretending to be a woman!

*As You Like It* is not the only play to rely on gender ambiguity to drive its storyline: In *Twelfth Night*, Viola disguises herself as a male page, Cesario. Here, theatre-goers would have been treated to a triple irony as Viola (boy actor dressed as a woman dressed as a man) falls in love with Orsino and in turn becomes the object of Olivia's affections. As in so many of Shakespeare's comedies, resolution is only finally achieved through the marriage of the protagonists: Viola to Duke Orsino and Lady Olivia to Viola's twin brother Sebastian.

In *The Two Gentlemen of Verona*, Julia and her maid Lucetta travel to Milan disguised as men in pursuit of Julia's erstwhile lover Proteus. Still in disguise, Julia contrives to be hired as Proteus' page. Only a fainting fit and the recognition of a love token in the form of a ring given to her by Proteus reveals her identity and reconciles the two lovers.

Falstaff is the only major male character in Shakespeare to subvert gender norms. In *The Merry Wives of Windsor* he is tricked by Mistress Ford into dressing up

## Gross Gourmets, Part II

A second famously grim list of ingredients goes into the pot in the notorious witches scene in *Macbeth* Act IV, scene i. Here the witches use:

- Poisoned entrails,
- 'Toad that under cold stone / Days and nights has thirty-one' (i.e. a toad that's a month old)
- 'Sweltered venom, sleeping got' (snake venom that's been sweated out in sleep)
- 'Fillet of a fenny snake' (fillet of a snake that lives in either a fen or marshland)
- 'Eye of newt'
- 'Toe of frog'
- 'Wool of bat' (bat hair)
- 'Tongue of dog'
- 'Adder's fork' (the forked tongue of an adder)
- 'Blind worm's sting' (venom from a slow-worm — actually without venom in real life)
- 'Scale of dragon'
- 'Witch's mummy' (fragments of a mummified witch)
- 'Maw and gulf / Of the ravined salt sea shark' (the stomach and gullet of a shark that's just finished eating its prey)
- 'Root of hemlock digged i' the dark' (root of hemlock, a plant well known for its poisonous properties, dug up

during the night when its poison was thought to be at its strongest)

- 'Liver of blaspheming Jew' (see racism and anti-Semitism; anti-Semitism appears to have been a recurring feature of some of Shakespeare's plays)
- 'Gall of goat' (gall, secreted by the liver)
- 'slips of yew/Slivered in the moon's eclipse' (slices of the yew tree, also poisonous, cut during an eclipse of the moon, a particularly inauspicious time)
- 'Nose of Turk' (similar to the 'blaspheming Jew' in that a Turk would also not have been christened)
- 'Tartar's lips' (as above, but an inhabitant of the Russian and Mongolian steppes instead of a Turk)
- 'Finger of birth strangled babe/Ditch-delivered by a drab' (finger of a baby strangled at birth, delivered by a prostitute in a ditch)
- 'A tiger's chaudron' (tiger's entrails)
- 'Baboon's blood' (the baboon was considered to be especially lecherous)
- 'Sow's blood that hath eaten/ Her nine farrow' (nine being a particularly inauspicious number)
- 'Grease that's sweaten/From the murderer's gibbet' (grease accumulated on a gibbet from the corpse of a convicted murderer)

as her maid's corpulent aunt, the fat woman or witch of Brentford. Falstaff gets a sound thrashing for his pains, while Sir Hugh Evan's comment: 'I spy a great peard [beard] under his muffler' suggests the gender bending is probably best left to the boy actors in Shakespeare.

Other gender benders include Portia in *The Merchant of Venice* – who takes the name Balthasar in her disguise as a lawyer from Rome – and Imogen in *Cymbeline*, who in hiding from her husband, takes on the disguise of Fidele.

## FAILED SUICIDES, PART I

In *King Lear*, Edgar, disguised as the mad vagrant Poor Tom, describes the seven ways he has been tempted to suicide and thus damnation by the devil. He has been:

- Led through fire and flame
- Led through rivers (i.e. 'through ford and whirpool')
- Led over bogs and quagmires

- The devil has 'laid knives under his pillow'
- The devil has laid 'halters in his [Tom's] pew' (i.e. ropes with which to hang himself)
- The devil has 'set ratsbane [ie poison] by his porridge'
- He has been 'made proud of heart, to ride on a bay trotting horse over four-inched bridges to course his own shadow for a traitor' (i.e. the devil has tempted him to ride over dangerously narrow bridges in pursuit of his own shadow)

Christian folklore had ratsbane, knives and halters as the traditional gifts of the devil to those in despair. It was held to be in the devil's interest to tempt people to kill themselves since it was believed a suicide's soul would go straight to hell.

## FAILED SUICIDES, PART II

In Act IV of *King Lear*, the Earl of Gloucester tries to commit suicide by jumping off a cliff. In a moment of dark irony, he is prevented from doing so by Edgar his son – who earlier, disguised as Poor Tom, had described being tempted to suicide by the devil. In the event, the blind Gloucester is tricked into believing he has jumped off a cliff and somehow survived when in fact he has only fallen to his knees. As before, the theme of being tempted to suicide by the devil is made explicit. Gloucester is led to believe that 'some fiend' had taken him to the top of the cliff. Edgar describes the fiend as having eyes like 'two full moons', a thousand noses and 'horns welked and waved like the enridged sea'.

## Most Difficult To Stage, part I

It's not always easy to stage Shakespeare – indeed, sometimes it seems the playwright goes out of his way to make things difficult for directors. *All's Well That Ends Well*, for example, has a notoriously problematic final scene in which Bertram instantaneously switches from loathing Helena his wife to loving her in the space of a single line. On discovering that she has tricked him into sleeping with her he relinquishes a whole play's worth of vitriol in a moment, promising to 'love her dearly, ever, ever dearly'.

Another very notorious scene occurs in *The Winter's Tale*, after Antigonus is charged with the killing of Hermione's infant daughter. Here, his abandoning of the baby on the shores of Bohemia is followed with the infamous stage direction: 'Exit pursued by a bear.' An intriguing possibility is that a live animal was used in the original productions: bear baiting was certainly a popular sport in the sixteenth and seventeenth centuries and there were bear-baiting arenas in the vicinity of the Globe and Rose theatres. Modern directors, however, tend to opt for the actor-in-a-bear-suit solution to the dilemma.

Another late play, *Cymbeline*, has an equally problematic stage direction. Posthumus, wrongly jailed for rebelling against the king and siding with the Romans, is visited in his sleep by the ghosts of his brothers, mother and father. Their appeal to Jupiter for justice is met with the following stage direction:

*Jupiter descends in thunder and lightning, sitting upon an eagle; he throws a thunderbolt.*

After chastising the ghosts for meddling in earthly affairs Jupiter ascends once more to the heavens on his eagle. Again, we have pretty much no idea how this would have been staged in Shakespeare's time.

## POISONINGS PART I: HAMLET

*Hamlet* is the granddaddy of all Shakespeare's poison plays. No less than four characters are done away in the final scene through the combination of a poison-tipped sword and a poisoned chalice:

I)   Gertrude, the queen, drinks from the poisoned chalice. Her last words are: 'The drink, the drink! I am poison'd.'

II)   Claudius, the evil king who has murdered his own brother for the crown, is stabbed with the poisoned rapier by Hamlet and then given a taste of his own medicine when forced by his nephew to drink poison from the chalice. His last (ironic) words are: 'O, yet defend me, friends. I am but hurt.'

III) Laertes, brother to drowned Ophelia and son to murdered Polonius, dies after being stabbed by Hamlet with his own poisoned rapier. He confesses his part in the poison plot and points the finger of blame at the king: 'Lo, here I lie, / Never to rise again. Thy mother's poisoned. / I can no more. The King, the King's to blame.'

IV) Hamlet, meanwhile, is stabbed by Laertes and dies from the poison on the rapier. His final words: 'The rest is silence.'

## POISONINGS PART II: OTHER POISONINGS

We've already seen how *Hamlet* contains no less than four on-stage poisonings. There is, however, a more significant poisoning that, despite taking place before any of the action begins, is actually the catalyst for everything that happens subsequently: that of Old Hamlet, the king. In Act I, scene v of the play, the ghost of the king describes how he has been killed by the 'juice of cursed hebenon', hebenon being the folk name for henbane, the juice of the plant *Hyoscyamus niger*. He then goes on to relate how he was poisoned and describes the grisly action of the henbane on his body, lines worth quoting in full if only for grim effect:

> Swift as quicksilver it courses through
> The natural gates and alleyways of the body,
> And with a sudden vigour it doth posset
> And curd, like eager droppings into milk,
> The thin and wholesome blood. So did it mine.
> And a most instant tetter barked about,
> Most lazar-like, with vile and loathsome crust
> All my smooth body.

The image is of blood being curdled by the poison (a posset was a drink made from milk curdled by wine or ale) and the king's skin becoming covered in a scabby crust ('barked about') like a leper's.

Shakespearean lore has it that this incident was inspired by the real-life murder of the Duke of Urbino in 1538 after his barber rubbed poisoned lotion into his ears. Incidentally, henbane was used in 1910 by notorious killer Hawley Harvey Crippen (better known as Dr Crippen) to murder his wife.

## DEMONS, FAMILIARS, WITCHCRAFT: KING LEAR

In *King Lear*, Edgar disguised as the madman Poor Tom describes how 'the foul fiend' 'follows' and 'vexes' him – then makes reference to the six spirits or demons that haunt him. The names are taken – some in a corrupted form – from Samuel Harsnet's *Declaration of Egregious Popish Impostures*, a treatise on witchcraft and possession published in 1603. Poor Tom's demons include:

**I. Flibbertigibbet**. The 'foul fiend' responsible, according to Poor Tom, for 'the web and the pin' (i.e. cataracts) and harelips. The demon also 'squenies the eye' (causes squints), 'mildews the white wheat' (causes almost ripe wheat to rot on the stalk) and 'hurts the poor creature of the earth'.

**II. Smulkin.** Also described as a 'foul fiend' by Poor Tom. He is the madman's 'follower', so could be his familiar or facilitator in the spirit world. In Harsnet's *Declaration*, Smulkin exits a possessed man's ear in the guise of a mouse.

**III. and IV. Modo and Mahu**. In Harsnet's Declaration, the two are generals at the head of demonic armies. In contrast, Poor Tom says they are alternative names for Satan: 'The Prince of Darkness is a gentleman; Modo he's called and Mahu'.

**V. Fraterretto.** Again, another name from Harsnet. Tom exclaims: '[He] calls me and tells me Nero is an angler in the lake of darkness'.

**VI. Hoppendance.** A corruption of Harsnet's Hoberdidance. In Lear, Tom characterises the demon as a toad hidden in his stomach: 'Hoppendance cries in Tom's belly for two white herring. Croak not, black angel! I have no food for thee.'

**VII. Obidicut**. Responsible for lust.

**VIII. Hobbididence**. The 'prince of dumbness'.

## DEMONS, FAMILIARS, WITCHCRAFT: MACBETH

It is not just Poor Tom in *King Lear* who has his familiars. In *Macbeth*, the witches also have their demonic followers. In Act I, scene i, the following exchange between the three takes place:

**First Witch:** I come, Greymalkin.
**Second Witch:** Paddock calls.
**Third Witch:** Anon!

Greymalkin and Paddock are usually glossed by editors as a grey cat and a toad respectively, while the 'anon' is sometimes interpreted as a response to the call of an owl – all three of which are traditional animal associates in witchcraft (think Hedwig the owl in *Harry Potter*, for a modern example).

## MOST DIFFICULT TO STAGE, PART II

It's not just the comedies and the 'problem plays' that offer staging dilemmas; the tragedies also have their own stock of difficulties.

The foremost of these in *Macbeth*, for example, is the march on Birnan Wood in Act V, scene iv where Malcolm's army chops down the branches of trees to disguise their numbers – thus fulfilling the witches' prophesy of Macbeth's downfall: 'Fear not till Birnan Wood/ Do come to Dunsinane'. The second staging dilemma is in the final scene in the play where Macduff 'enters with Macbeth's head'. Papier-mâché historians relate that 'japanning', the art of producing solid objects from mashed-up paper, only reached England in the mid-seventeenth century so it's an open question how Shakespearean prop managers would have dealt with this particular stage direction.

Another interesting and supremely gory staging challenge involves the putting out of the Earl of Gloucester's eyes in *King Lear*. Here the challenge is made all the greater by the fact that the earl has three acts of the play after his eyes have been put out to wander, blinded and bloodied, as the tragedy unfolds.

As in so many areas though, it is Shakespeare's supreme gore-fest *Titus Andronicus* that takes the plaudits in the most-difficult-to-stage stakes. Here, a single stage direction in Act II, scene iv causes all the problems:

*Enter the empress' sons with Lavinia, her hands cut off, and her tongue cut out, and ravished.*

For the remainder of the play, a mute, blood-spattered, deranged Lavinia staggers across the stage, her suffering a silent witness to the cruelty of Aaron, the Empress and her sons. Indeed, so difficult is this scene to stage that modern directors have often attempted more stylised or abstract stagings, replacing the blood with ribbons, for example, or absenting Lavinia from the action altogether. Sometimes, it seems, even Shakespeare goes too far.

## LITERARY CROSS-FERTILISATIONS: POETRY

As in film, novels and television, the world of poetry has witnessed its own fair share of Shakespearean borrowings.

**I. Robert Browning.** Nineteenth-century English poet Robert Browning was one of the leaders of this trend, taking lines from Shakespeare as a title for one of his better known poems. 'Childe Roland to the Dark Tower Came' finds its genesis in medieval literature but is also found in a muddled-up song by Edgar disguised as Poor Tom in *King Lear*:

> *Child Roland to the Dark Tower Came*
> *His word was still 'Fie, foh, and fum,*
> *I smell the blood of a British man'*

**II. Ogden Nash.** *Very Like a Whale*, a collection of nonsense poems by Ogden Nash, comes appropriately enough from Act III, scene ii of *Hamlet*, where Polonius is gulled into talking gibberish by Hamlet:

> **Hamlet:** Do you see yonder cloud that's almost in shape of a camel?... Methinks it is like a weasel.
> **Polonius:** It is backed like a weasel.
> **Hamlet:** Or like a whale.
> **Polonius:** Very like a whale.

**III. Robert Frost.** The title for 'Out, Out', a poem by Robert Frost comes from *Macbeth* Act V, scene i, where Lady Macbeth, driven mad by her part in Duncan's murder, attempts to wash away imaginary spots of blood from her hands: 'Out, damned spot! Out, I say!'.

**IV. Sylvia Plath.** A song from *The Tempest*, Act I, scene ii was the inspiration for the title of Sylvia Plath's 1958 poem 'Full Fathom Five'. In the original, the spirit Ariel taunts Ferdinand for the (as he believes) recent drowning of his father:

Full fathom five thy father lies;
Of his bones are coral made;
Those are pearls that were his eyes:

Lines from Ariel's song also appear in Books I and II of
T.S Eliot's 1922 masterpiece *The Waste Land*.

## CAPITALISING ON THE BARD

Forget Hamlet Cigars: the commercialisation of
Shakespeare has scaled ever greater heights since the
advent of the internet.

The Poor Yorick Shakespeare Catalogue at bardcen-
tral.com, for example, was until recently accepting
orders for a whole world of lovingly crafted
Shakespeare 'Toys and Doohickeys'. Among them
'deliciously strong wintergreen mints in a Shakespearean tin (My Kingdom for a wintergreen mint!)', an
Alas! Poor Yorick Mug ('Our Yorick skull-in-hand logo
on a hefty, 15 oz. ceramic mug with a large easy-grip
handle') and Shakespeare Stationery Cards ('Blank

note cards with sticker quotes featuring more than two dozen quotations and celebratory greetings for all occasions').

Other useful knick-knacks included a Bawdy Mug ('this mug is downright dirty, if you're in the know') and a Bawdy Pillow ('A true inspiration for your boudoir or Cheapside sitting room. 100% cotton and machine washable').

Or how about the Hamlet Finger Puppet Set ('Now you can be playwright, actor and director, putting on countless productions') or the Little Shakespeare Toy Figure ('Each of these posable figures comes with a collectable, twelve page, mini color comic book chronicling William's crazy adventures!')? Other options include the Shakespeare Action Figure ('Articulated 5" tall hard plastic William Shakespeare action figure with removable book and quill') and the Shakespeare Nodder ('To nod or not to nod, that is the question').

But pride of place surely has to go to the Shakespeare Little Thinker Doll, for which the advertising spiel runs: 'Are you tired of all those cute but essentially brainless "beanie" dolls? We were, so to offset the trend we designed the "Little Thinkers". Let the Little Thinkers add a little culture and humour to your life. 11" tall and oh, so smart!'

Unfortunately, the catalogue stopped accepting orders in December 2007. As a result, devastated Bard enthusiasts the world over have been forced to shop elsewhere for their memorabilia.

## BIG BROTHER

Ignorance of Shakespeare seems to be a pre-requisite for any appearance on a reality TV show and almost a formula for success. In Germany's first series of *Big Brother*, for example, one of the most popular participants in the show was called Zladko.

Zladko's ignorance was such that he became notorious for replying 'A shake beer?' when asked about Shakespeare. He didn't win the competition, but did make a hit single which went top-ten. The song contained the line: 'I don't give a f*ck about Shakespeare or Goethe'.

Likewise, in the 2007 UK version of the reality TV show, data entry clerk Brian was teased by his housemates for his ignorance of Shakespeare. When asked by *Big Brother* whether *Babe: Pig in the City* was written by Shakespeare, Brian replied: 'I don't know who this geezer is who's meant to have written or directed all these things. Think it's *Babe: Pig in the City*, because they spoke normal in that. I don't know how William Shakespeare directed it though.'

Despite this, researchers at the show later revealed that Brian had taken a GCSE in English and so would therefore have had at least some acquaintance with Shakespeare in one form or another. Whether Brian was therefore wilfully misleading his housemates about the depth of his ignorance of Shakespeare remains one of the great unsolved mysteries of the 2007 series.

## *What's Eating Iago?*

Iago in *Othello* has to be one of Shakespeare's nastiest characters. He dupes Roderigo out of his wealth, ruins Cassio's good name, stabs his own wife literally in the back and works Othello up into such a froth of jealous rage that he kills the utterly blameless Desdemona.

Critics have long been split about what exactly motivates Iago to act with such spite towards all those around him. There are, however, hints within the play – especially about his loathing for Othello. In Act I, scene iii he says he hates Othello because of rumours that the Moor has committed adultery with his wife, Emilia: 'It is thought abroad that 'twixt my sheets / He's done my office.' The same theme appears later in the play when he says:

> I do suspect the lusty Moor
> Hath leapt into my seat, the thought whereof
> Doth like a poisonous mineral gnaw my
> inwards

## WORST POETRY?

**Fourth citizen:** Tear him to pieces; he's
a conspirator!
**Cinna:** I am Cinna the poet, I am Cinna the poet!
**Fourth citizen:** Tear him for his bad verses, tear
him for his bad verses!

The above almost Pythonesque exchange takes place in *Julius Caesar* after the emperor's assassination. Here, mob rule even extends to literary criticism, it seems.

The final scene of another of the Roman plays, Coriolanus, gives birth to another potentially inappropriate and unintentionally Pythonesque moment:

**All Conspirators:** Kill, kill, kill, kill, kill him!
*[The Conspirators draw, and kill Coriolanus:]*
*[Aufidus stands on his body]*
**All Lords:** Hold, hold, hold, hold!

# WILL THE REAL
# WILL SHAKESPEARE
# PLEASE STAND UP ...

So who *really* wrote the plays?

Was it the philosopher Francis Bacon? Perhaps it was Shakespeare's contemporary, Christopher Marlowe. Or maybe it was even Sir Walter Raleigh or Elizabeth I. One of the great things about Shakespeare is that the relative scarcity of detail about his private life leaves us with a void that just begs to be filled with conspiracy theories about who he really was.

One such theory states there's no way that Shakespeare could possibly have written the plays. He was the son of a rural glove-maker – had never been to university, had never as far as we know even travelled further than London. How could such a man possibly have written with such insight, erudition and authority across such a broad spectrum of topics and genres? Only a thorough grounding in the classics, for example, would have prepared the way for a playwright to tackle *Julius Caesar*, *Antony and Cleopatra*, *Coriolanus* and *Titus Andronicus*. Shakespeare, according to contemporary playwright Ben Jonson, had 'but little Latin and less Greek'.

Likewise, in an age where most of the rural population barely ventured more than a few miles further than their home village, how could a native of sleepy Stratford know enough to base 22 of his plays in locations far outside the British Isles? The same argument runs true for the intimate knowledge of courtly rituals on display in Shakespeare's plays – and what about the playwright's evident familiarity with contemporary theories on witchcraft and the occult (see *Macbeth* and *King Lear*, especially)? Then there are the frequent references to theology and the bible, an awareness of foreign languages (Latin in *Love's Labour's Lost* and French in *Henry V* in particular, for example), an understanding of astrology and an apparent intimacy with the workings of the legal world.

Given these apparent deficiencies in background, it's no surprise that modern academics have dredged up a surfeit of candidates for the 'real Shakespeare'...

# THE REAL WILL SHAKESPEARE?

### *Edward de Vere*

One of the candidates for the 'real' Shakespeare, according to scholarly naysayers, is Edward de Vere, the 17th Earl of Oxford who was not only well travelled, wealthy and educated, but also had a fledgling literary career that was mysteriously cut short just as Shakespeare's got under way. Here the critical verdict ranges from 'plausible' to 'no way!' with apparently little common ground in between. The verdict? This has potential but the theory has been widely ridiculed by the academic establishment.

### *Francis Bacon*

A second candidate for the 'real' Shakespeare is Francis Bacon, the ultimate renaissance heavyweight whose interests ranged from philosophy to alchemy, theology to politics. Vastly erudite, well travelled and well connected; Bacon would certainly have had the background and the knowledge to have taken a stab at writing the odd play or two. Conspiracists have also found cryptograms in Shakespeare that could point towards Bacon as the author. One such is an anagram in the made-up word *honorificabilitudinatibus* in *Love's Labour's Lost*, which can be rearranged to read: hi ludi F. Baconis nati tuiti orbi and translated as 'these plays F. Bacon's offspring preserved for the world'. Given this apparent weight of evidence, the generally accepted verdict on the Bacon-as-Shakespeare theory is that it is plausible but unlikely: apart from anything else, Bacon was phenomenally productive in his own right without having the time to pen 30 or so plays of his own.

### Kit Marlowe

A third candidate for the 'real' Shakespeare is Christopher 'Kit' Marlowe, the 007 of the Elizabethan theatrical world. Not only was Marlowe a wonderfully talented playwright but he also allegedly did a bit of spying on the side – a consideration that adds sufficient spice to the story to make conspiracy theorists drool. The argument runs that Marlowe's mysterious death in a pub brawl in 1593 was a cover-up, and that the playwright - because of the necessity of maintaining the fiction of his death – was obliged to write under the

Shakespeare pseudonym from then on. Here, the verdict on Marlowe-as-Shakespeare is that it's plausible – other than the inconvenience of having to account for the plays already written by Shakespeare ahead of Marlowe's death in 1593.

## Other possibilities

Other notable candidates for the 'real' Shakespeare include (in decreasing order of probability): William Stanley, Earl of Derby; Ben Jonson; Thomas Middleton; Sir Walter Raleigh, and finally Queen Elizabeth I.

So who was the real Shakespeare? Perhaps Ralph Waldo Emerson came closest in *Shakespeare; or, the Poet* in 1904 when he wrote: 'Shakespeare is the only biographer of Shakespeare; and even he can tell us nothing.'

# MUSICAL ADAPTATIONS

## Twelfth Night

*Twelfth Night* has been subject to a couple of rock-opera re-renderings. *Your Own Thing* was a Summer-of-Love retelling that premiered off-Broadway in 1968. Featuring such timeless rock classics as 'No-one's Perfect, Dear', 'The Flowers', 'Somethin's Happenin' (Baby! Baby!)', 'Hunca Munca', and 'The Now Generation'. The musical revolves around 20-year-old twins, Viola and Sebastian, who, as in the Shakespearean original, are victims of mistaken identity. After they are separated in a shipwreck, Viola disguises herself as a man to audition for an all-male rock quartet 'The Apocalypse', whose lead singer – Disease – has been drafted to fight in the Vietnam War. Hilarity ensues as Sebastian is mistaken for Viola and vice versa before the confusion is resolved and the twins find their true loves.

The original production of *Your Own Thing* ran for a remarkable 937 performances at the Orpheum Theater, off Broadway. It also opened in London's West End and in Sydney, Australia.

A second musical remake came in the form of 2005's juke-box offering *All Shook Up*, which ran for 213 performances at the Palace Theatre on Broadway. The plot revolved around the same is-she-a-he-or-is-she-a-she theme, but this time weaved songs by Elvis Presley into the action. Unfortunately, the show got a less than flattering first-night review from *New York Times* theatre critic Ben Brantley who – clearly jaded by rock musical adaptations – wrote: 'What you have just heard is the sound of a camel's back breaking.'

## Hamlet

Hard to credit, but 1994's Disney offering *The Lion King* has been cited as a musical reworking of Hamlet. Here, Simba's succession issues and his anxiety about his place within the 'Circle of Life' are said to mirror Hamlet's own Oedipal dilemmas. Unlike *Hamlet*, however, *The Lion King* had both a sequel and a part prequel/part-midquel (*The Lion King 1 ½* and *The Lion King II: Simba's Pride*) as well as an award-winning score featuring Elton John.

## The Comedy of Errors

*The Boys from Syracuse*, taking *The Comedy of Errors* as its inspiration, wins plaudits as the first musical adaptation of a Shakespeare play. Featuring lyrics by Lorenz Hart and music by Richard Rodgers, it debuted on Broadway at the Alvin Theater on 23 November 1938 and ran for 235 performances. Song titles include 'I Had Twins', 'Dear Old Syracuse', 'Let Antipholus In' and 'Oh, Diogenes!'

## Love's Labour's Lost

Kenneth Branagh's 2000 version of *Love's Labour's Lost* may have deserved some recognition for being the first musical adaptation of Shakespeare's most difficult and inaccessible play – but it was still roundly panned by critics. Among the reviewers' less favourable comments were 'unfathomably awful' (David Edelstein), 'smug' (Kenneth Turan), 'inadequate in every way' (Stanley Kauffmann).

Less critical, however, was *Variety* reviewer Derek Elley, who wrote of the film: 'Anyone with an open mind and a hankering for the simple pleasures of Tinseltown's Golden Age will be rewarded with 90-odd minutes of often silly, frequently charming and always honest entertainment.' Despite this, the film was a flop.

## The Taming of the Shrew

Cole Porter's musical *Kiss Me, Kate* is by far the most successful musical adaptation of a Shakespeare play, sweeping the 1948 Tony Awards with Best Musical, Best Author of a Musical, Best Composer and Lyricist, Best Costume Design, and Best Producer of a Musical. It ran for a record 1,077 performances after opening on Broadway at the New Century Theatre on 30 December 1948.

MISOGYNY: PART I

A lot of it about in Shakespeare but perhaps the most savage example of misogyny falls from the deranged mind of King Lear when meditating on the unnatural lusts of his less-than-kind daughters:

> *Down from the waist they are centaurs,*
> *Though women all above;*

*But to the girdle do the gods inherit,*
*Beneath is all the fiends' -*
*There's hell, there's darkness, there is the sulphurous pit -*
*burning, scalding, stench consumption! Fie, fie, fie! Pah,*
*pah!*

## MISOGYNY: PART II

Like King Lear, *Cymbeline's* Posthumus Leonatus has a splendidly jaundiced view of women. He utters the following observations after being duped into believing his wife Imogen has been unfaithful with the dastardly Iachimo.

The faults he ascribes to women are: 'lying', 'flattering', 'lust and rank thoughts', 'revenges', 'ambitions', 'covetings', 'changes of prides', 'disdain', 'nice longing', 'slanders' and 'mutability'. He adds:

All faults that may be named, nay, that hell knows,
Why, hers, in part or all; but rather, all.

## GOOD IN BED?

Is Cleopatra the best shag in Shakespeare? She might be if Enobarbus is to be believed. In the following, Maecenas is pointing out the necessity of Antony leaving Cleopatra for Caesar's sister Octavia. Enobarbus explains why it won't happen:

> Never; he will not:
> Age cannot wither her, nor custom stale
> Her infinite variety: other women cloy
> The appetites they feed: but she makes hungry
> Where most she satisfies.

## WAS SHAKESPEARE A RACIST?

It's not nice and it shouldn't be sugar-coated but racism is hard to avoid in Shakespeare. Critics point out that Shakespeare's empathy with the persecuted in plays such as *Othello* and *The Merchant of Venice* actually provides insight into how corrosive racism is – and that this insight therefore ultimately carries an anti-racist message. At the same time it's hard to get away from the fact that a contemporary Shakespearean audience would have been far removed from any modern multi-cultural mindset and so probably wouldn't have had much empathy for any 'outsiders' in the plays.

Regardless of how you interpret its meaning or intent, however, racism crops up most explicitly in *Othello*, *The Merchant of Venice*, *Titus Andronicus* and *The Tempest*.

## *Othello*

In *Othello*, the central character, a Moor of African descent, is defined by his skin colour: in the eyes of his enemies it – and a beast-like lust – become his defining characteristics. In Iago's words, he is a 'black ram' 'tupping [Brabantio's] white ewe', he is a 'Barbary horse', he is described as 'the thick lips' and 'a devil'.

According to one reading, it's Othello's status as an outsider that makes him so susceptible to Iago's machinations. In one key passage, where he first plants the seeds of doubt about Desdemona's fidelity in Othello's mind, Iago deftly plays on the Moor's ignorance of and insecurity about Venetian society:

I know our country disposition well:
In Venice [wives] do let God see the pranks
They dare not show their husbands; their best conscience
Is not to leave't undone, but keep't unknown

### What's Eating Othello?: Jealousy

*Othello* offers an unparalleled study into the destructive nature of jealousy. It also offers up some extremely quotable lines on the subject.

In Act III, scene iii of the play, for example, Iago, Othello's Machiavellian advisor, warns against feelings of jealousy:

O! Beware, my lord, of jealousy;
It is the green-eyed monster which doth mock
The meat it feeds on.

In the same scene after Iago has sown the seed of doubt about Desdemona's fidelity, Othello says:

I had rather be a toad,
And live upon a corner of dungeon,
Than keep a corner in the thing I love
For others' uses.

In Act III, scene iv, Iago's wife
Emilia observes:

Jealous souls will not be answered so;
They are not ever jealous for the cause,
But jealous for they are jealous.

By the end of the play, of course, the green-eyed monster triumphs, bringing in train the deaths of Desdemona, Emilia, Roderigo and Othello, the wounding of Cassio and the removal of Iago to the dungeons to be tortured until he either dies or confesses his guilt.

## The Merchant of Venice

The Merchant of Venice is another play that for modern audiences has a problematic attitude towards race. Here, and in common with Othello, Shylock is first and foremost an outsider. In the court scene at the play's culmination, for example, he is referred by his name just six times and as 'Jew' a full 22 times. The audience is left in little doubt that it is partly his Jewishness that drives his desire for revenge against Antonio and his 'pound of flesh'. Anyone 'worth the name of a Christian', we feel, would have opted for a far more reasonable arrangement.

## Titus Andronicus and The Tempest

In Act IV, scene ii of Titus Andronicus, Aaron, a Moor, fathers an illegitimate son who is described by its nurse as 'A joyless, dismal, black, and sorrowful issue' and 'as loathsome as a toad'. The child's mother, the Empress, fearful that the Emperor will discover her infidelity, persuades the nurse to tell Aaron to 'christen [the child] with thy dagger's point' (ie murder it). Aaron resists, however, declaring: 'Zounds, ye whore! Is black so base a hue?/Sweet blowse, you are a beauteous blossom, sure.'

Later in the same scene he makes a passionate defence of his blackness:

Coal-black is better than another hue,
In that it scorns to bear another hue...

In *The Tempest*, meanwhile, Caliban is described as 'this thing of darkness' and remains throughout the play an outsider, a malignant force, because of his 'deformity' and skin colour.

Racist language also crops up in *Love's Labour's Lost*, where King Ferdinand, the King of Navarre, states that 'Black is the badge of hell, the hue of dungeons and the scowl of night'. Likewise, in Act II, scene v of *The Two Gentlemen of Verona* Launce tells Speed: 'If thou wilt go with me to an alehouse so; if not, thou are a Hebrew, a Jew, and not worth the name of a Christian'.

*Richard II*, *Henry IV Part II*, *Antony and Cleopatra*, *The Merry Wives of Windsor*, *Much Ado About Nothing* and *Macbeth* also have their own examples of racist language.

## *What's Eating Aaron?*

Like Iago in *Othello*, Aaron in *Titus Andronicus* is the author of some of the nastiest and most vindictive plots in Shakespeare. He not only convinces the Empress' sons to rape and maim Lavinia, but tricks Titus into lopping off his own arm in the vain hope of saving his sons from execution. If anything, Aaron's motives are even harder to fathom than Iago's. In Act V, scene i he tells Lucius how he duped Titus into cutting off his own arm and then: 'drew myself apart/ And almost broke my heart with extreme laughter'. Later in the same scene he outlines what has to be the most tasteless practical joke imaginable, exclaiming:

> Oft have I digg'd up dead men from their
> graves,
> And set them upright at their dear friends'
> doors,
> Even when their sorrows almost were forgot;
> And on their skins, as on the bark of trees,

Have with my knife carved in Roman letters,
'Let not your sorrow die, though I am dead.'

Thoroughly unrepentant, among the other 'notorious ills' he has practised are: killing or devising how to kill, raping or plotting how to rape, accusing the innocent of crimes they haven't committed and setting friends at odds. He has also made 'poor men's cattle break their necks' and 'set fire on barns and haystacks in the night, / ... bidd[ing] the owners to quench them with their tears'. Aaron: a thoroughly nasty piece of work.

# BLOOD AND GORE: MACBETH

Gore figures large in *Macbeth* – especially immediately after the murder of Duncan. In Act II Scene ii, Macbeth enters 'carrying two blood-stained daggers'; he refers to his 'hangman's hands', before Lady Macbeth tells him to get water 'to wash [off] this filthy witness'. Later in the same scene Macbeth begins to fear the blood will never be cleaned and that oceans would turn red before it came away:

> Will all great Neptune's ocean wash this blood
> Clean from my hand? No, this my hand will rather
> The multitudinous seas incarnadine,
> Making the green I red.

Lady Macbeth then smears the hands and faces of Duncan's sleeping grooms with the dead king's blood to implicate them as the murderers. Macbeth is later confronted by the bloody ghost of Banquo – who he has had murdered – while his queen goes mad, spending her final hours before committing suicide attempting to wash imaginary spots of blood from her hands.

## BLOOD AND GORE: JULIUS CAESAR

The assassination of Julius Caesar in the play that bears his name is accompanied with enough gore to satisfy the most bloodthirsty of theatregoers. In Act II, scene i, after Caesar has been stabbed to death (he receives a more than sufficient 33 stab wounds), Brutus urges his co-conspirators to cover themselves with the dead man's blood:

> Let us bathe our hands in Caesar's blood
> Up to the elbows, and besmear our swords:
> Then walk we forth, even to the market place…
> waving our red weapons o'er our heads.

## BLOOD AND GORE: CYMBELINE

*Cymbeline* has its own unexpectedly gory moments. Imogen, awaking from a deep, drug-induced sleep, finds the headless corpse of what she believes to be her husband beside her. Unaware that it is in fact the decapitated body of her nemesis Cloten she daubs herself with the corpse's blood.

## BLOOD AND GORE: TITUS ANDRONICUS

*Macbeth*, *Julius Caesar* and *Cymbeline* may all have their moments, but for all their blood-letting, the play with far and away the most gore has to be *Titus Andronicus*. Severed limbs galore, rape, ripped out tongues, attempted infanticide and two lead characters cooked in a pie serve to make for probably the most gruesome viewing on the Elizabethan stage.

## *What's Eating Edmund?*

Dashing but entirely lacking in moral scruples, Edmund in *King Lear* is the archetypal philanderer and his roguish credentials are unparalleled by any other character in Shakespeare. Not only does he seduce two queens, the queens he seduces are sisters to each other. On hearing about the suicide of Goneril and the poisoning of Regan he even appears to hint at the potential for a diabolical post-death ménage a trois: 'I was contracted to them both. All three / Now marry in an instant'.

In the play, Edmund's wickedness seems to be driven firstly by the fact of his illegitimacy but also by a lust for power. Even his death-bed repentance goes against the grain of his character, as he himself admits:

I pant for life; some good I mean to do
Despite of mine own nature.

## OUCH! MOST STABBED CHARACTER IN SHAKESPEARE

According to Octavius, Julius Caesar's body receives 33 stab wounds. Cassius, Casca, Brutus, Decius, Cinna, Metellus Cimber and Trebonius are among the culprits.

## THE FATE OF KINGS

Kings and queens have a hard time in Shakespeare. Time and again in the history plays the playwright exercises his fascination with majesty: its burdens and rewards. More than occasionally kings and queens come to a sticky end. Perhaps Richard II expresses it best just ahead of his meeting with Bolingbroke, his exiled usurper:

Let us sit upon the ground,
And tell sad stories of the death of kings -
How some have been disposed, some slain in war,
Some haunted by the ghosts they have disposed,
Some poisoned by their wives, some sleeping killed.

All murdered - for within the hollow crown
That rounds the mortal temples of a king,
Keeps death his court

## Some of the less fortunate kings include:
**Richard III** (dies on the battlefield)
**Duncan** (assassinated)
**Lear** (dies of old age and shock)
**Macbeth** (killed then beheaded on the battlefield)
**Hamlet's father** (poisoned by his own brother)
**Richard II** (killed by Exton, who mistakes
Bolingbroke's off-the-cuff comments for a
death-warrant)
**Henry VI** (stabbed to death by Richard III)

## Some unfortunate queens include:
**Cleopatra** (commits suicide by asp)
**Regan** (poisioned by Goneril)
**Goneril** (commits suicide by stabbing herself)
**Gertrude** (drinks from the poisoned chalice of wine
intended for Hamlet. Dies exclaiming: 'The drink,
the drink! I am poison'd.')

## INCEST PART I

Yes, even incest has its place in Shakespeare. Not content with littering his plays with beheadings, hangings, poisonings, drownings and stabbings, the Bard also chooses plots where some of his characters partake of some pretty dubious sexual shenanigans too. In *Pericles*, Antiochus, the king of Antioch, and his daughter are engaged in a secret incestuous relationship. Pericles guesses what is happening and flees the country before Antiochus can have him put to death for fear of his revealing the secret.

Pericles describes how the king 'with foul incest' partakes of 'actions blacker than night':

Where now you're both a father and a son,
By your untimely claspings with your child
(Which pleasure fits a husband, not a father);
And she an eater of her mother's flesh.

Eventually father and daughter get their comeuppance, of course: both are struck and killed by lightning.

## INCEST PART II

In *Hamlet*, there is more than just a suggestion that Claudius' relationship with Gertrude is incestuous in that he is the brother of her dead husband. That a Shakespearean audience would have found such couplings offensive is clear from the 1563 *Table of Kindred and Affinity*, where people related – even through wedlock – were forbidden 'in scripture and [the] laws' from marrying. Thus it is that the king's description of his new wife – whom he has married barely a month after murdering her husband – as 'sometime sister, now our queen' would have been considered especially distasteful. The same distaste is behind Hamlet's lament for his mother's eagerness to be bedded by the king in 'incestuous sheets'. The ghost, meanwhile, characterises Claudius as 'that incestuous, that adulterate beast' and warns his sons to 'Let not the royal bed of Denmark be / A couch for luxury and damned incest'. At the same time, 20th-century critics especially have been quick to point out that there is more than a hint of an Oedipus complex in Hamlet's speech in the famous scene where he confronts his mother. Freud's *The Interpretation of*

*Dreams*, published in 1900, led the way with a view that Hamlet has an 'Oedipal desire for his mother and the subsequent guilt [prevents] him from murdering [Claudius], who has done what he unconsciously wanted to do'.

## ALL MEN ARE BASTARDS

At least that's what seems to be implied by Balthazar's song in Act II, scene iii of *Much Ado About Nothing*:

Sigh no more, ladies, sigh no more,
Men were deceivers ever,—
One foot in sea and one on shore,
To one thing constant never.

In *Cymbeline*, Posthumus Leonatus comes to the same conclusion – 'We [men] are all bastards' – but for totally different reasons. His conclusion is that all men are essentially bastards because of the infidelity of their mothers.

## SCOTTISH NATIONALISM

Macduff's 'O Scotland, Scotland!' (Act IV, scene iii) in *Macbeth* is the nearest Shakespeare comes to any expression of Scottish patriotism. Perhaps it's unsurprising that *Macbeth* is pro-Scot: it was written for James I, England's first Scottish king.

Most of the other plays are less flattering: Scotland is generally seen as a hotbed of insurrection and as a nuisance that fosters instability. In *Henry IV, Part II*, for example, the traitor Northumberland escapes to Scotland until 'time and vantage' allow him to muster enough strength to face the king again; while in *Henry V*, the Earl of Westmoreland talks of 'the weasel Scot' and of the need to defend England against a Scottish invasion.

## BASTARDS

There are a lot of bastards in Shakespeare – bastards in the traditional sense, obviously, in that they were born outside of marriage; but actually a good few of them are bastards in the modern sense of the word too.

Among the good bastards are the Bastard of Orleans, one of the French leaders in *Henry VI, Part I*, and Philip (the Bastard) Faulconbridge from *King John*.

Among the bad bastards are Don John, the dastardly brother of Don Pedro in *Much Ado About Nothing*, and Edmund in *King Lear*. Edmund is probably the biggest bastard of the lot: not only does he dally with the affections of two sisters, he causes his own father to be tortured and to have his eyes pulled out, orders faultless Cordelia to be hanged and tries to kill his own brother.

In *Cymbeline*, meanwhile, Posthumus Leonatus comes to the unhappy conclusion that: 'We [men] are all bastards' after being fooled by the evil Iachimo into believing his wife Imogen has been unfaithful to him. He bitterly observes: 'That most venerable man which I/ Did call my father was I know not where/ When I was stamped.'

One other type of bastard in Shakespeare: in *Henry IV, Part I*, Hal describes Falstaff's enjoyment of bastard, a type of sweetened wine from Spain.

## COD LATIN?

The character of Pistol in *Henry IV, Part II* has some splendid muddled lines of faux latin. In Act II, scene iv he gives his motto as *Si fortune me tormente sperato me contento*, which translates as 'If fortune torments me hope contents me'. By the fifth act of the same play the phrase has become: *Si fortuna me tormenta, spero me contenta*.

## Gross Gourmets, Part III

Shakespeare's *Titus Andronicus* wins the prize for leaving the worst taste in the mouth when it comes to gross gourmets, featuring as it does a truly unpleasant act of cannibalism.

In revenge for the killing of his two sons and for the raping and maiming of his daughter, Titus turns the Empress' sons Chiron and Demetrius into the main ingredients for a pie to be served at a banquet in her honour. He uses his one remaining good hand to slit the throats of the two men, while his daughter Lavinia holds 'tween her stumps' the basin that collects their blood. He outlines his recipe for the pie as follows:

Receive the blood: and when that they are dead,
Let me go grind their bones to powder small
And with this hateful liquor temper it;
And in that paste let their vile heads be baked.

In the final, bloody scene of the play, he enters dressed as a cook, and when asked the whereabouts of Chiron and Demetrius declares:

Why, there they are both, baked in that pie;
Whereof their mother daintily hath fed,
Eating the flesh that she herself hath bred.
'Tis true, 'tis true; witness my knife's sharp point.

His next act is to stab the horrified Empress – presumably with the same knife he used to slit the throats of her wicked sons.

## SWORDS AS SWEETHEARTS

In much the same way as Wild West gunslingers might have developed an affection for their six-shooters, Shakespearean swashbucklers can display an unhealthy attachment to their weapons. *In Henry IV, Part II*, faux swaggerer Pistol gently lays down his sword with the words: 'And, sweetheart, lie thou there!'

## SHEEP'S GUTS

*Twelfth Night*'s 'If music be the food of love' is one famous quote about music in Shakespeare. In Act II, scene iii of *Much Ado About Nothing*, Benedick has a far more cynical take on the ability of music to fire the imagination: 'Is it not strange that sheep's guts should hale souls out of men's bodies'. Here, sheep's guts are the material with which Renaissance instruments would have been strung.

## COLDEST WORDS IN SHAKESPEARE

*'I know thee not, old man.'*

Said by Hal to Falstaff on their first meeting after Hal's coronation as Henry V. Hal casts off any associations with his one-time boon buddy and the world he inhabits, making it clear that Falstaff should:

Presume not, that I am the thing I was,
For heaven doth know (so shall the world perceive)
That I have turn'd away my former self,
So will I those that kept me company.

## SADDEST WORDS IN SHAKESPEARE

For lovers of Falstaff, Shakespeare's larger-than-life lecherer, drinker and loveable rogue, the following might just qualify as the saddest words in Shakespeare:

'Master Shallow, I owe you a thousand pounds.'

The line is spoken by a crestfallen Falstaff to Justice Shallow, from whom he has borrowed on the expectation of preferment under Hal, straight after he has been rejected by the new king. It is literally the first and only time in any of the plays that we see the hitherto untouchable Falstaff at a loss for words and utterly impotent in the face of a setback. Significantly, it is also the only time we ever see him admitting to owing someone else money; in all other instances he has attempted to bamboozle his creditors. The play ends with a sadder, feebler Falstaff being thrown into the Fleet Prison by his nemesis, the Lord Chief Justice, preparing the way for his death in *Henry V*.

# 'I HAVE DONE THE DEED': WORST STAGINGS OF SHAKESPEARE

Peter O'Toole's *Macbeth* at the Young Vic in 1980 is often described as the worst production of any major Shakespeare play in recent times. Of particular note was O'Toole's appearance on stage in Act II, scene ii after the murder of Duncan, literally covered from head to foot in blood. The single line: 'I have done the deed' is said to have been met with gales of laughter from the nonplussed audience.

O'Toole's predecessor in the 'worst stagings' stakes has to be 19th-century sensation Robert Coates, a Shakespearean actor who was so bad that crowds flocked to theatres to witness his dreadful improvisations and bombastic renderings of well-known scenes. Coates is said to have been so convinced of his own genius that he would often repeat the death scenes in which he appeared or invent new dialogue on the spur of the moment in an effort to 'improve' the original. Unfortunately, his fame couldn't last: audiences eventually tired of his overblown performances and he died in obscurity in 1848 after being hit by a Hansom cab.

## SHAKESPEARE'S BED

An inordinate amount of space and time has been devoted to scholarly discussions on the question of Shakespeare's bed. The reason for this is the entry in Shakespeare's will that reads: 'Item, I give unto my wife my second best bed with the furniture'. Clearly, this begs the question: why did he leave his wife only his second best bed and who got the best bed? The generally accepted answer is that the best bed was reserved for guests to the house, whereas the second best bed is where Shakespeare and his wife would usually have slept.

## STABBINGS: PART I

Anyone who thinks stabbings and street violence are a something new doesn't know the sixteenth and seventeenth centuries, at least if Shakespeare's plays are any kind of guide. Loads of characters in the plays get stabbed – often either by being assassinated or through mortal combat. They pretty much all die. Here are just a few of the more memorable ones:

## I. Duke of Clarence *(Richard III)*
Stabbed then drowned in a vat of wine containing the severed heads of pigs.

## II. Richard II *(Richard II)*
The deposed king is stabbed by Exton who mistakes an off-the-cuff comment by the new king for a death warrant.

## III. Coriolanus *(Coriolanus)*
Aufidius, leader of the Volscians, incites a group of conspirators to kill the Roman leader. The final scene contains his stabbing and death.

## IV. Henry VI *(Henry VI, Part III)*
Done away with in the Tower of London by the dastardly Duke of Gloucester, soon to become Richard III. Henry VI's indignities don't end there, however: Gloucester later seduces his widow, Lady Anne, over his dead body (literally).

## V. Julius Caesar *(Julius Caesar)*

Caesar's stabbing is probably the harshest: his 'Et tu, Brute' has entered the language as the stock response to an outrageous betrayal.

## VI. Richard III *(Richard III)*

Richard III gets his comeuppance for his murderous misdeeds on Bosworth field where he is killed by The Earl of Richmond, later Henry VII.

## VII. Hotspur *(Henry IV, Part I)*

The fiery Hotspur, son to the Duke of Northumberland, meets his match in a redeemed Prince Hal on the battlefield at Shrewsbury.

## VIII. Edmund *(King Lear)*

Edmund, arguably the nastiest piece of work in *King Lear*, meets his end in a duel with Edgar, the brother he slandered earlier in the play. Good triumphs over evil, making for an unlikely deathbed *volte face* from Edmund as he repents his many sins.

### IX. Emilia *(Othello)*
Reveals details of the plot against Othello and is stabbed in the back by her thoroughly evil husband, Iago. Dies singing a song about willows.

### X. Lavinia *(Titus Andronicus)*
Wins the award for the most put-upon character in Shakespeare: not only is her husband murdered in front of her, she raped and mutilated; she is also stabbed by her own father in the climactic scene of the play.

### XI. Tamora *(Titus Andronicus)*
Gothic queen stabbed to death with a butcher's knife by the long-suffering Titus in the final scene of the play. She dies with the knowledge that she's eaten her own sons after they were baked in a pie and served up to her by Titus.

### XII. Titus Andronicus *(Titus Andronicus)*
Eventually even Titus gets his chips. The Emperor Saturninus stabs him after learning of the meat pie plot. He in turn is stabbed by Lucius, Titus' son.

## THE MOST ALCOHOLIC DEATH

The award for the most alcoholic death in Shakespeare goes to George, Duke of Clarence, who, in *Richard III*, ends his days drowned in a large barrel of malmsey wine.

## SUICIDE

Suicide was a very big deal in the sixteenth and seventeenth centuries. Anyone taking their own life would be denied a Christian burial and a place in heaven – to commit suicide was to be eternally damned. Contrary to popular belief, there are more than the oft-quoted unlucky thirteen suicides in Shakespeare's plays:

**I.** Romeo and Juliet kill themselves: Romeo by poison; Juliet by stabbing herself. (2)

**II.** In *Julius Caesar*, Cassius convinces his servant Pindarus to assist him in committing suicide, and Brutus runs on to a sword held by his servant Strato. In the same play, Brutus' wife Portia kills herself by swallowing hot coals. Titinius stabs himself. (6)

**III.** Othello stabs himself after learning of Desdemona's innocence. (7)

**IV.** In *Hamlet*, Ophelia's death is initially characterised as an accident by the Queen, however, as the play progresses it becomes increasingly clear that Ophelia has taken her own life after being driven mad by Hamlet's rejection of her and his murder of Polonius, her father. In Act V, scene i, the priest says her death was 'doubtful' and that - but for the order of the king - she would not receive a Christian burial. (8)

**V.** Lady Macbeth's death in Act V is also considered a suicide. Malcolm describes how the 'fiend-like' queen 'by self and violent hands / Took off her life'. (9)

**VI.** Another queen, Goneril in *King Lear*, kills herself. (10)

**VII.** The self-neglect of Timon in *Timon of Athens* can

be taken as a form of suicide. Disillusioned by the hypocrisy of his false friends he withdraws from society and at the end of the play is found dead in a cave - an apparent suicide. (11)

**VIII.** But the play with the biggest suicide count is *Antony and Cleopatra* with a grim tally of five self-inflicted deaths. Eros, a follower of Antony, stabs himself rather than obey Antony's order to kill him. Antony is then left to kill himself. Charmian and Iras, Cleopatra's followers, also kill themselves rather than contemplate a life without their mistress. But the award for most glamorous suicide probably goes to Cleopatra, whose asp-induced death goes down in Bardolatry as one of the most melodramatic and best. (16)

**IX.** Finally, Cordelia's death in *King Lear* is an example of an attempted faked suicide. Edmund gives orders that the old king's daughter should be hanged and her death be made to look like suicide. He says: '[The captain] hath commission from... me / To hang Cordelia in the prison, and / To lay the blame on her own dispair,/ That she fordid herself.'

# HANGINGS

Bardolph is one of Falstaff's boon buddies in *Henry IV, Part I* and *Henry IV, Part II*. In *Henry V* the king makes an example of Bardolph to deter the English soldiers from looting: he is hanged for stealing a woolen pax.

A hanging also lies in wait for the unfortunate Clown in *Titus Andronicus* when he delivers pigeons and letters to Saturninus. Death on a rope is all the thanks he gets for his troubles.

Probably the saddest hanging though is that of Cordelia in *King Lear* who is hanged on the orders of the dastardly Edmund. Even a last-minute reprieve on the orders of a dying and repentant Edmund is not enough to save her: she dies in the arms of her father; the reprieve coming an instant too late.

## BEHEADINGS

The Duke of Somerset appears among the Lancastrian faction in *Henry VI, Part II*. His head is carried onstage by Richard (later Richard III) in the opening scene of *Henry VI, Part III*.

Macbeth is killed in a sword fight by Macduff, who then appears holding the king's severed head aloft.

In *Cymbeline*, Cloten has his head cut off by Guiderius.

## STABBINGS: PART II

More Shakespearean stabbings, including those from the sword-fests *Macbeth*, *Romeo and Juliet* and *Hamlet*:

### I. Duncan (*Macbeth*)

Candidate for the goriest stabbing, Duncan's violent death in Act I resonates through the remainder of the play: in Macbeth's fear that 'all great Neptune's ocean' will not wash the blood from his hands and in Lady

Macbeth's frantic and deranged attempts to wash imaginary blood from her hands in Act V.

## II. Banquo *(Macbeth)*
Banquo and his son Fleance are set upon by three murderers in the pay of erstwhile friend Macbeth. While Fleance flees, Banquo cops it.

## III. Lady Macduff *(Macbeth)*
More murderings at Macbeth's behest. Lady Macduff is last seen exiting stage left after witnessing her son being stabbed by the King's murderous cronies.

## IV. Macbeth *(Macbeth)*
What goes around comes around in the final scene of the Scottish Play: Macbeth meets his nemesis Macduff and is slain after learning that his opponent was 'from his mother's womb/ Untimely ripped'.

## V. Mercutio *(Romeo and Juliet)*
Mercutio is the first casualty of a play intensely preoccupied not just with young love but also with swordfighting and duelling. He is stabbed by Tybalt as Romeo

attempts to separate them.

### VI. Tybalt *(Romeo and Juliet)*
Tybalt's death follows Mercutio's in short shrift as Romeo revenges the death of his silver-tongued companion.

### VII. Paris *(Romeo and Juliet)*
Romeo gains another feather in his duelling cap with the death before Juliet's tomb of Paris. All three eventually end up dead in the tomb along with the corpse of Tybalt, Juliet's cousin.

### VIII. Polonius *(Hamlet)*
The first death of many in this soliloquy-laden Shakespeare classic. Has the honour of being the only Shakespearean character to be stabbed while hiding behind a curtain.

### IX. Laertes *(Hamlet)*
Keen to revenge the death of his father and the drowning of his sister, Laertes takes on Hamlet in a duel. Is stabbed by his own poisoned rapier.

**X. Claudius** *(Hamlet)*
The fratricidal king gets a taste of his own medicine when stabbed with a poisoned rapier by his own nephew, Hamlet.

**XI. Hamlet** *(Hamlet)*
Meets his maker at the point of the same poisoned rapier he uses to stab and kill Laertes.

# FAMOUS LAST WORDS

'Et tu, Brute? Then fall, Caesar!'
**Julius Caesar**

'The rest is silence.'
**Hamlet**

'As sweet as balm, as soft as air, as gentle, O Antony!
Nay, I will take thee too. What should I stay?'
**Cleopatra**

'Thus with a kiss I die.'
**Romeo**

'Commend me to my kind lord. O! farewell!'
**Desdemona**

'Killing myself to die upon a kiss...'
**Othello**

'A horse! A horse! My kingdom for a horse!'
**Richard III**

'And damn'd be him that first cries, 'Hold, enough!'
**Macbeth**

'The drink, the drink; I am poison'd!'
**Queen Gertrude**

'Look on her, look, her lips, Look there, look there!'
**King Lear**

'Demand me nothing; what you know, you know:
From this time forth I will never speak a word.'
Iago's last words before being carted off to be tortured
in *Othello*.

In *Henry IV, Part I,* Harry 'Hotspur' Percy doesn't
even get to finish his dying speech. It's left to Hal to
provide the concluding word: 'worms':

'Thought's the slave of life, and life time's fool;
And time, that takes a survey of all the world,

Must have a stop. O! I could prophesy,
But that the earthy and cold hand of death
Lies on my tongue. No Percy, thou are dust,
And food for ...

# EPITAPH

Shakespeare's epitaph appears over his tombstone in the chancel of Stratford's Trinity Church:

*Good friend, for Jesus´ sake forbeare*
*To digg the dust enclosed here.*
*Blest be ye man that spares thes stones*
*And curst be he that moues my bones*

# SHAKESPEARE'S PLAYS: HAVE YOU SEEN THEM ALL?

All's Well That Ends Well

Antony & Cleopatra

As You Like It

The Comedy of Errors

Coriolanus

Cymbeline

Hamlet

Henry IV, Part i

Henry IV, Part ii

Henry V

Henry VI, Part i

Henry VI, Part ii

Henry VI, Part iii

Henry VIII*

King John

Julius Caesar

King Lear

Love's Labour's Lost

Macbeth

Measure For Measure

Merry Wives of Windsor

A Midsummer Night's Dream

Much Ado About Nothing

Othello

Pericles

Richard II

Richard III

Romeo & Juliet

The Taming of the Shrew

The Tempest

Timon of Athens

Titus Andronicus

Troilus & Cressida

Twelfth Night

Two Gentlemen of Verona

The Two Noble Kinsmen*

The Winter's Tale

*probably written in collaboration with (or later revised by) John Fletcher, a member of Shakespeare's dramatic company.

# ACKNOWLEDGEMENTS

To Soph for putting up with me and for Monty for when he's old enough to read. Thanks to BenB for suggestions and to Luke for beer and sympathy. Also big thanks to Tom and Anova for advice and for knocking it all into shape.

Quotes from the plays from:
http://www.opensourceshakespeare.org

Euphemisms from Eric Partridge's excellent 'Shakespeare's Bawdy'.

# BLANK VERSE